The Russo-Chinese Borderlands

Zone of Peaceful Contact or Potential Conflict?

by W. A. DOUGLAS JACKSON

Professor of Geography
University of Washington

A SEARCHLIGHT ORIGINAL
under the general editorship of

GEORGE W. HOFFMAN
University of Texas

G. ETZEL PEARCY
United States
Department of State

D. VAN NOSTRAND COMPANY, INC.
PRINCETON, NEW JERSEY

TORONTO   LONDON

NEW YORK

D. VAN NOSTRAND COMPANY, INC.
120 Alexander St., Princeton, New Jersey
(*Principal Office*)
24 West 40 Street, New York 18, New York

D. VAN NOSTRAND COMPANY, LTD.
358, Kensington High Street, London, W.14, England

D. VAN NOSTRAND COMPANY (Canada), LTD.
25 Hollinger Road, Toronto 16, Canada

Published simultaneously in Canada by
D. VAN NOSTRAND COMPANY (Canada), LTD.

PRINTED IN THE UNITED STATES OF AMERICA

Preface

For about 4500 miles the Union of Soviet Socialist Republics (USSR) and the People's Republic of China (CPR) meet each other along an oft-proclaimed "friendship" boundary that carves a broad arc across Asia from the Pamir "roof" to the chilly waters of the Pacific (Map 1). Today, a degree of stability, perhaps hitherto unknown, characterizes the lands through which this boundary marches. The friendship which is reflected therein between the peoples of Russia and China is cited by Communist theorists as proof of the thesis that between socialist countries conflict is not only not possible, now or ever, but that all wars result from the competition among or the imperialism of the capitalist countries. Ideological solidarity would seem, therefore, to account for the present calm along the international boundary.

Sino-Soviet friendship has created a new political-geographical situation in Asia. It is interesting to recall, for a moment, that the actual boundary between these two immense states achieved its present exactitude only in the period 1945-49. It had been in the making for over three centuries and came about simply as a result of the expansion of both Russia and China, each in search of its own "final frontier."

The most recent change in this long historic process occurred in 1944, when the Soviet Union surreptitiously incorporated Tannu Tuva (already a Soviet satellite but formerly part of Outer Mongolia and thus of Imperial China) into the USSR as the Tuvinian Autonomous Oblast. But Russian expansion at the expense of China came to an end when the Communists seized control of Peking. The event forced a reassessment of Soviet strategy in Asia, but at the same time the victory of Communism in China gave the Soviets an ideological ally in the Far East.

The ties between the USSR and the CPR have resulted in bringing much of Eurasia, from the western border of East Germany to the southern border of North Viet Nam, under Communism. The Russo-Chinese borderlands, which historically had been zones of tension, have become stabilized. Rather than dividing Russia and China, they now serve to link these two major Communist powers. Indeed, for the first time in modern history, the Heartland of Eurasia lies within the control of forces hostile to the Western democracies. This political-geographical situation is one which, a half century ago, Sir Halford Mackinder, the British geographer, warned against. He believed that possession of the Heartland would give the possessor enormous advantages which could lead ultimately to world domination. However, Mackinder did not, even as late as World War II—nor, it should be noted, did anyone else—envisage that the Heartland would fall under Sino-Soviet control.

The full significance of these developments is not readily seen, and there are many questions which remain to be answered.

Will the ideology of Communism, dedicated to the overthrow of all non-Communist governments, outweigh over the long run all other considerations of purely national interest and advantage? Or, to what extent in the future will the divisive force of egocentric nationalism serve to alienate from each other these disciples of Marx and Lenin? In the latter case, should we expect the present boundary between the USSR and the CPR to be the "final" boundary and the status quo of the borderlands to be preserved?

These questions, of course, deeply concern the peoples of the West. We may not, to our satisfaction, find the answers, but our search for understanding will, in no small way, help us in preparing to meet the further challenge of twentieth-century international Communism.

This text is concerned primarily with the history and political geography of the lands along the Russo-Chinese international boundary. Throughout modern times Russia has been the expansionist power, while China was the "sick man" of Asia. Consequently, much of the study focuses on those traditional Chinese territories—Manchuria, Mongolia, and Sinkiang—which, until the Communist victory in China, were much coveted by the Russians, Tsarist or Soviet. Today, Manchuria and Sinkiang are unquestionably Chinese, but Mongolia, though independent, remains more closely associated with Moscow than with Peking. It is, therefore, mainly with respect to Mongolia that many of the questions above are raised. Some Western observers see Mongolia as a potential issue between Russia and China, whereas others view the question as relatively unimportant in the light of over-all international Communist strategy. It is hoped that this brief examination of the borderlands will not only introduce the reader to these little-known, but fascinating regions, but also shed further light on the nature of the Sino-Soviet relationship.

The author is indebted to Dr. Roy Wolfe, a geographer with the Department of Highways, Province of Ontario, who, as Visiting Professor at the University of Washington in 1960-61, offered many helpful suggestions in the initial preparation of the text, and to Professor Norton Ginsburg of the University of Chicago, who read several chapters to the author's advantage. The interpretation of the role of the Russo-Chinese borderlands in Russian and Chinese history, however, is the author's, and he bears sole responsibility for the errors.

Seattle, Washington   W. A. Douglas Jackson
January, 1962

Contents

List of Maps

I *The Zone of Contact*

IN ORDER to understand more clearly the present Sino-Soviet borderlands and their role in the world today, it is useful to divide them into three geographical sectors: Inner Asia, Mongolia, and the Far East.

The Inner Asian sector, extending for some 2000 miles from the lofty Pamirs in the south to the Altai Mountains in the north, involves the steppes and deserts of Turkestan. The boundary itself cuts rather arbitrarily over mountains and valleys. To the west lies Western or Russian Turkestan, now known as Soviet Central Asia; to the east is Eastern or Chinese Turkestan, or Sinkiang, recently renamed the Sinkiang-Uighur Autonomous Region (Map, p. 2), after the Uighurs, the largest ethnic group.

East of the Inner Asian sector is the Mongolian sector. Here the Mongolian People's Republic (MPR), or Outer Mongolia, lies between the USSR and the CPR, preventing immediate geographical contact between them. The Soviet-Mongolian boundary stretches for about 1500 miles eastward from the Altai Mountains over mountains and uplands into the plateau of Trans-Baikalia. The Sino-Mongolian boundary begins in the Altai and ends in Trans-Baikalia also, but only after extending in a broad concave arc across the Gobi Desert. However, from 1921 to 1955, when Soviet hegemony over Mongolia was almost total, the southern boundary of the republic was, *de facto,* the boundary between Russia and China. Following the Communist revolution in China and Peking's formal recognition of Outer Mongolia's independence, the status of the MPR began to change, a development which in turn affected the nature of Mongolia's boundaries.

1

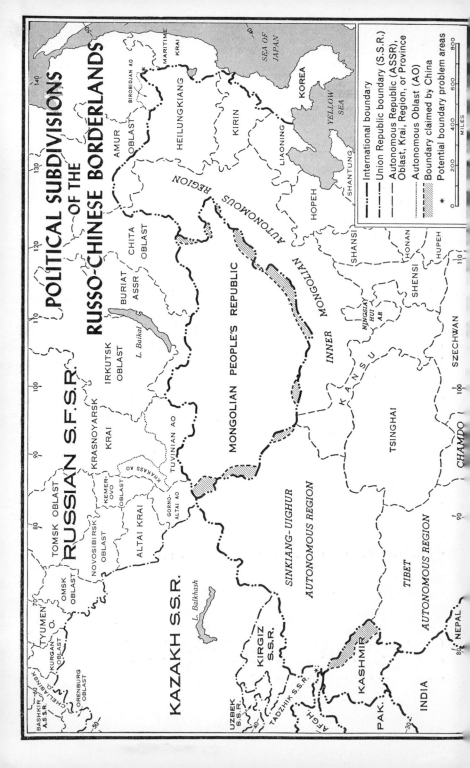

The final sector of the borderlands falls within the Far East and, to a considerable extent, occupies the basin of the Amur. Indeed, the Amur and its tributaries, the Argun and Ussuri, form the boundary separating Eastern Siberia and the Soviet Far East from the Chinese Northeast Region or Manchuria.

THE INNER ASIAN SECTOR

The division of ancient Turkestan between Russia and China was effected by a series of treaties drawn up between 1860-81, following the respective occupations of the territory by both powers. Although the Russians, both before and after the Bolshevik Revolution, crossed into Sinkiang for political or economic advantage, the international boundary has remained unchanged for almost a century. According to contemporary Chinese maps, however, the delineation across the Pamir plateau is still to be determined. Earlier (pre-1953) Chinese maps had been drawn with the boundary several hundred miles to the west of the present location, thus including a large part of the plateau within Sinkiang.

The Pamir region, as a study of the map will reveal, is indeed a strategic one (Map, p. 4). To the south lies Afghanistan and beyond it, Kashmir, which is disputed between India and Pakistan. The Russian boundary with Afghanistan was demarcated by a joint Anglo-Russian commission in 1895 leaving Wakhan in Afghan hands as a buffer between the Russian and British Empires. At one point, the airline distance between Russia and Kashmir across Wakhan is only eight miles. On the Indo-Pakistani side, however, the Wakhan valley is buttressed by the mighty Hindu Kush (Mountains), which rise to 25,000 feet.

The presence of British troops in the subcontinent—and of the British fleet beyond—guaranteed the stability of the Pamir boundaries. This power was removed in 1948 when Pakistan and India emerged as independent states, and their joint strength since has been lessened as a result of their conflict over Kashmir. While no evidence exists of a direct threat to Pakistan from the USSR, the Russians have at least encouraged secessionist feeling among the Pathans who live in Pakistan's northwest. On the other hand, there

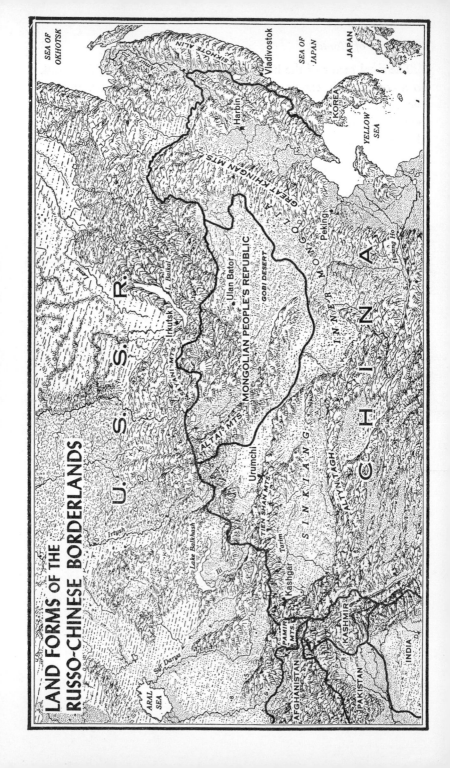

LAND FORMS OF THE RUSSO-CHINESE BORDERLANDS

is sufficient proof of China's ambitions to cause alarm throughout the entire subcontinent. Much attention has been focused on the Chinese-Indian boundary dispute that developed in 1959 following the discovery that the Chinese Communists had built a road across India's Outer Ladakh linking Sinkiang and Tibet. It should be noted that the Sino-Pakistani boundary is also disputed by the Chinese. Should the Chinese Communists gain control of the major mountain passes through the Karakorum Range connecting Sinkiang with Pakistan's Gilgit Agency, a serious threat to Pakistan's very existence as an independent state could develop.

The Pamirs have been described as the roof of the world. To the late Soviet geographer, L. S. Berg, they were "a miniature Tibet" where the ranges reach 16,000 to 18,000 feet in elevation. Snow lies on the higher peaks all year round, but it is for the most part a dry barren land. Yet it was up over these lofty mountains from Kashmir that the 13th century Venetian traveller, Marco Polo, came on his remarkable journey to the fabled court of Kublai Khan, nephew of Genghis Khan.[1]

The present Sino-Soviet boundary through the eastern Pamirs, as shown on Soviet maps, is probably not far to the east of Marco Polo's route. The Soviet Pamir lies within the Gorno-Badakhshan Autonomous Oblast, a subordinate unit of the Tadzhik Soviet Socialist Republic. The Tadzhiks are ethnically related to the Iranians as well as to some of the peoples to the south in Afghanistan. Although the Tadzhik Republic has nearly two million inhabitants, the bulk of the population lives in the valleys of the Vaksh and Amu-Darya Rivers to the west, leaving the high plateau sparsely occupied.

Marco Polo probably followed an old trail across the plateau, but today a motor road makes travel less tedious. Until recently there was no motor road through or into the Chinese Pamirs, but in the last few years the Chinese Communists have built a road southwest from Kashgar to Puli, 200 miles distant. Known as the Pamir Road, it heads ominously in the direction of the Karakorum passes and Pakistan's Gilgit Agency. Puli is the capital of the Tash Kurghan Tadzhik Autonomous Hsien, a subordinate ethnic administrative

[1] *The Travels of Marco Polo,* New York: Boni and Liveright, 1926, p. 66.

area in Sinkiang whose inhabitants are Sarikola Tadzhiks and, as Ismaeli Muslims, followers of the Aga Khan.

The Sino-Soviet boundary runs northward from the Pamirs into the Trans-Alay Ranges, which bound the Pamirs in the north. Beyond the ranges lies a broad upland valley, drained primarily to the west by the Kyzyl-Su. Much of the upland territory through which the boundary passes has been occupied for centuries by Kirgiz nomads. Its administration is now divided between the Kirgiz SSR, on the one hand, and the Chinese Kirgiz Autonomous Chou, or district, on the other.

From the upland valley, the Sino-Soviet boundary turns eastward into the Tien-Shan where, for the most part, it follows the crest of the Kokshaal-Tau Range. The Tien-Shan, extending for nearly 2000 miles in an east-west direction through Inner Asia, are a mass of ranges of varying ages, containing small enclosed valleys (Map, p. 2). The highest peak lies in the central Khan-Tengri Range (23,000 feet), which marks the boundary between Russia and China. A major break in the Tien-Shan, permitting movement across the Sino-Soviet boundary, is the Torugart Pass at 12,700 feet. Marco Polo, on his way to Kashgar, descended into the Tarim Basin by way of the pass, which is now crossed by a motor road.

On the Soviet side, the Tien-Shan fall primarily within the Kirgiz SSR, but the largest and most fertile valley in the complex lies to the west within the Uzbek SSR. The Uzbeks, a Turkic people, have long been sedentary and possess a strong state tradition. Thus, for centuries the Fergana Valley, watered by the Syr-Darya and its major tributary, the Naryn, has been an important center of culture and irrigated crop cultivation. As a result of the construction of the Stalin Great Fergana Canal in the 1930's, Fergana's position as the major cotton-producing region of the USSR was further strengthened. Eastward, in Sinkiang, the Tien-Shan, known to the Chinese as the "Heavenly Mountains," constitute a major geographic feature and, as Owen Lattimore suggests, "the key to Chinese Turkestan." [2] A highly complex mountain mass, the Tien

[2] Owen Lattimore, *Inner Asian Frontiers of China,* New York: American Geographical Society, 1940; 2nd edition, 1951, p. 151.

Shan divide Sinkiang in two. To the north lies Dzhungaria; to the south is the Tarim Basin.

The larger Tarim Basin is one of the driest regions of Asia. Indeed, it could be said that the extensive Takla-Makan which occupies the core of the basin is nearly rainless, owing to the barrier against moisture-bearing winds presented by the high mountains that border it on the south (Kun Lun), on the west (the Pamirs), and on the north (Tien-Shan). Yet, life has ancient roots in the Tarim Basin, focused on the oases that are widely scattered around the huge wasteland at the base of the mountains. Glacier-fed streams descending from the mountains and, to some extent, connected by the Tarim River have brought water, which has sustained life. Kashgar is the most important oasis, but Yarkend and Khotan beneath the lofty Kun Lun, and Aksu beneath the Tien-Shan, are also significant. Today Kashgar, with over 100,000 inhabitants, is the westernmost city of modern China and the administrative capital of southwestern Sinkiang, which has a total population of around three million. Because of the aridity, nomadic life is confined to the encircling uplands and involves such groups as the cattle-breeding Tadzhiks and Kirgiz pastoralists. In the oases, the predominant ethnic group is the Uighurs, a Turkic people (Map, p. 8). Although the name "Uighur" is an historic one, it was officially adopted only in 1921. Until that date, these Turkic peoples called themselves Kashgarians, or Khotanians, after the locality in which they lived. The number of Chinese in the Tarim basin, though increasing, is still thought to be relatively small, consisting mainly of administrative and military personnel.

Several motor roads through the high mountain passes to the west link the Tarim Basin with the Soviet Union. The oasis settlements at the feet of the encircling mountains are also linked by roads. Extending eastward along the base of the Altyn Tagh from the city of Kashgar, as mentioned previously, is the Silk Road, which Marco Polo followed on his way to Peking. Passing salty Lob-Nor in the eastern part of the territory, he moved into China through the Kansu Corridor. In those days, the Road permitted the exotic wares of the Orient to be carried to the Mediterranean. Recently, the Chi-

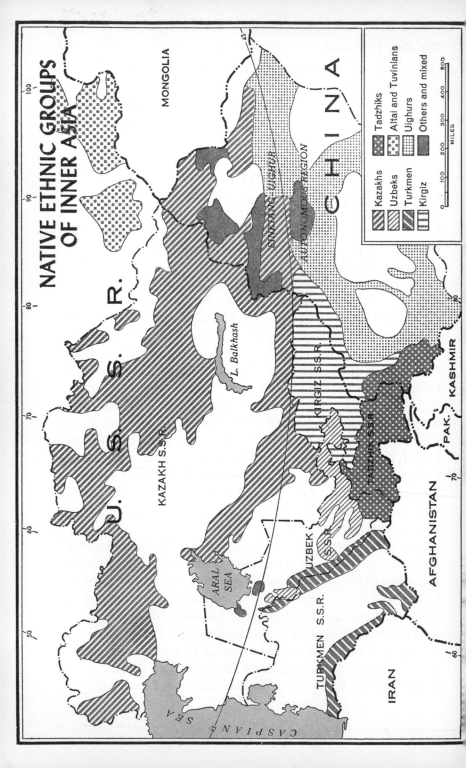

NATIVE ETHNIC GROUPS OF INNER ASIA

Kazakhs	Tadzhiks
Uzbeks	Altai and Tuvinians
Turkmen	Uighurs
Kirgiz	Others and mixed

MILES
0   100   200   300   400   500

MONGOLIA

U. S. S. R.

CHINA

KAZAKH S.S.R.

L. Balkhash

SINKIANG-UIGHUR AUTONOMOUS REGION

KIRGIZ S.S.R.

TADZHIK S.S.R.

UZBEK S.S.R.

ARAL SEA

TURKMEN S.S.R.

CASPIAN SEA

IRAN

AFGHANISTAN

PAK.   KASHMIR

50   60   70   80   90   100

nese Communists have built a railway through the historic corridor in an effort to develop the resources and economy of Sinkiang. A similar historic road, known as "The Dry Run", marches along the southern piedmont of the Tien-Shan, but at the eastern end of the mountains it turns north into the Turfan Depression. There it joins the Dzhungarian Road, which links Urumchi and Hami to the Kansu Corridor. Urumchi is the major city of Sinkiang, while Hami is the easternmost. These roads are to be improved, and parallel rail lines are to be laid sometime in the future. Finally, south from Kashgar the Communists have built the previously mentioned motor road through Outer Ladakh, claimed by India, into Tibet.

Approaching the Ili River, the Sino-Soviet boundary next crosses the "corridor area" of Inner Asia (Map, p. 4). Greater precipitation and moisture north of the Tien-Shan than to the south, and the presence of an almost continuous belt of good pastures along the northern slopes of the mountains, have made possible the large movements of nomads that have contributed so much to the shaping of the history of the peoples to the west. It was through these gates, in the 13th century, that the Mongol tribes under Genghis Khan came. Boundaries that cross corridors, particularly if they are river valleys, have traditionally been militarily vulnerable. The highways of western Dzhungaria demonstrate this fact most dramatically. Indeed, as General Kuropatkin, administrator of Russian Turkestan, noted in 1917, the most vulnerable part of the entire Russian frontier with China lay in the Inner Asian sector.

Immediately to the north of the main mass of the Tien-Shan lies the Ili valley, enclosed by the Narat and Borokhovo Ranges. Confined by the ranges at its eastern end, the basin widens toward the west, causing it to be more accessible to Russia than to China. The Ili, rising inside Sinkiang, drains into Lake Balkhash in Soviet Kazakhstan, nearly a thousand miles to the west. Not far inside the USSR, to the south of the Ili on the Turkestan-Siberian Railway, sits Alma-Ata, the capital of the Kazakh SSR. Founded by the Russians a century ago, it contains over 456,000 inhabitants, mainly Russian. From its position, the city is able to command the western approach to the upper Ili. The largest city on the Chinese Ili is Kuldja, a fortress town, with a population well over 110,000. The territory around Kuldja has been organized as the Sibo Autonomous Hsien, although the Sibos, a Tungus-Manchurian people, number only 19,-000. Because of their close association with the Uighurs and other Turkic peoples, the Sibos have been strongly Turkicized. In the past, the Ili was used by the Chinese government as a region of exile for political dissenters.

From Kuldja a good motor road leads westward into Soviet Kazakhstan and terminates at the Turk-Sib Railway. The distance from Kuldja to the Soviet railhead is only 200 miles, but until recently a three-month caravan trip was necessary to reach the nearest Chinese station 1200 miles to the east. Another motor road leads northward over the Borokhovo Range into the Dzhungarian Basin, where it meets the main Dzhungarian road. The Ili River also functions as a trade artery, the navigational season extending from the end of March to the beginning of November. Although the motor road across the boundary offers the advantage of direct shipping, in recent years the Ili has, nevertheless, carried from 25 to 35 thousand tons of freight. This tonnage includes agricultural machinery, cement, iron ore, and also oil.

North of the Ili Basin, the Sino-Soviet boundary climbs into the Dzhungarian Ala-Tau, an east-west trending range that reaches elevations of over 15,000 feet. Following the crest of the range, the boundary drops abruptly into a deep, low-lying depression, 46 miles long bounded on the north by the Barlik Maili Range. This is the historic Dzhungarian Gate. By way of Lakes Ebi-Nur and Alakol, it is in direct line with the major oases of Dzhungaria and, to the west of the international boundary, Lake Balkhash. Although the Dzhungarian Gate has not played an important role in modern times, it has been selected, according to present Sino-Soviet plans, as the route of the first Inner Asian transcontinental rail line linking Moscow to Peking.

Not far to the northeast, but beyond the Barlik Maili, the boundary again crosses open steppe. Here a good motor road, passing Chuguchak, affords connection between the main centers of Dzhungaria and Ayaguz on the Turk-Sib Railway. North of Chuguchak lies the Tarbagatai Range. The boundary extends into the mountains, turning east to follow, at 9800 feet, the crest of the eastern half of the range. From there it runs north across the valley of the Black Irtysh before reaching the piedmont of the Altai. The Black Irtysh River, rising in the Mongolian Altai to the east, drains into Lake Zaisan in the USSR, from whence the waters flow to the Arctic Ocean via the Irtysh and, finally, the Ob. The Black Irtysh is an important route for the transport of minerals and other goods from the northwest part of Sinkiang to the Soviet Union. A motor road runs through the valley, but its significance as an artery of Russo-Chinese commerce is considerably less than that of the southerly routes, because the country through which it passes is dry and sparsely occupied.

Dzhungaria is a triangular-shaped basin occupying over 270,000 square miles. On the northeast it is bounded by the Mongolian Altai, on the south by the Tien-Shan, and on the west it is blocked, as we have seen, by several isolated ranges. With a precipitation of from 8 to 10 inches per year in the lowlands and more in the uplands, Dzhungaria is able to support a larger pastoral population than the Tarim Basin to the south. Most of the 475,000 nomadic Kazakhs of Sinkiang live in the western uplands of Dzhungaria (Map, p. 8). In past times of crisis, the Kazakhs freely migrated back and forth from Russian to Chinese territory. Thus, the Sinkiang Kazakhs share a common history, as well as a common Turkic language with Russian Kazakhs. Though Muslims, they have traditionally been lax in observing the practices of Islam. Mongol pastoralists are scattered throughout the region, though there are concentrations in the north near the border of the MPR, as well as in the Tien-Shan to the south. Their religion, derived from Tibet, is Lama Buddhism.

The minority status of both Kazakhs and Mongols has been recognized by the Chinese Communists in subordinate ethnic administrative units. In addition to Kazakhs and Mongols, there are also large numbers of Uighurs, particularly in the oasis cities of Manass and Urumchi, as well as in Hami. Dzhungaria has at least 200,000 Dun-

Table I *Population of Sinkiang and Soviet Central Asia*
Sinkiang (1953)

I. Turkic peoples
   1. Uighurs or Eastern Turks 3,640,000
   2. Kazakhs 475,000
   3. Kirgiz 70,000
   4. Others 13,000
II. Chinese peoples
   1. Chinese 300,000
   2. Dungans (Muslims) 200,000
III. Mongols 120,000
IV. Manchus, Sibos, etc. 20,000
V. Russians 13,000
VI. Tadzhiks 15,000
VII. Others 8,000

                                              Total 4,874,000

Soviet Central Asia (including Kazakhstan) (1959)

I. Turkic peoples
   1. Kazakhs 3,193,000
   2. Uzbeks 5,961,000
   3. Kirgiz 955,000
   4. Turkmen 981,000
   5. Kara-Kalpaks 168,000
   6. Tatars 780,000
   7. Uighurs 74,000
II. Eastern Slavic peoples
   1. Russians 6,265,000
   2. Ukrainians 1,035,000
   3. Byelorussians 108,000
III. Dungans 10,000
IV. Koreans 213,000
V. Tadzhiks 1,378,000
VI. Others
   Jews 94,000
   Poles 53,000
   Armenians 20,000

                                            Total 21,218,000

Total Population given in Soviet Census of 1959
for the five republics 22,978,000

Sources: *East Turkic Review,* No. 4, 1960, p. 81; *Narodnoe khoziaistvo SSSR
v 1959 godu. Statisticheskii ezhegodnik* (Moscow, 1960, pp. 17-20).

gans, or Chinese Muslims. While the Chinese have never appeared in Sinkiang in great numbers (Table 1), in recent years more than a million have migrated to Dzhungaria from the eastern provinces. Urumchi, the chief industrial city of Sinkiang, has grown to 200,000; Hami has at least 100,000 inhabitants. Many Chinese are settling along the Manass River, where irrigation facilities are being expanded. The oilfields at Tushantzu and Karamai will undoubtedly afford a further stimulus to development.

Nevertheless, the Chinese in their development of Sinkiang have a long way to go to catch up with their Soviet counterparts in Central Asia to the west. Hitherto, change has come slowly to the region. Indeed, for most of the native peoples, life prior to 1950 probably had not departed radically from patterns dating back for centuries. On the other hand, whatever economic development there has been in the exploitation of resources and stimulation of trade occurred largely under the direction of Russians, who have at times assumed effective economic control.

Soviet Central Asia, in contrast, has experienced almost forty years of Communist rule. The entire region, including Kazakhstan, has been effectively integrated into the Soviet Union. Moreover, Russians and Ukrainians have migrated in considerable numbers into the area. Of the ethnic groups in Soviet Central Asia listed in the Soviet All-Union Census of 1959, Russians and other Eastern Slavic peoples account for over 7 million, the Turkic peoples about 12 million. In the cities, the centers of administration and industrial development, Russians form large minorities if not outright majorities. At any rate, control lies with the Russians, in the Communist Party and in Moscow. Separatist feeling among the native peoples has been suppressed whenever it appeared, and Islam, the traditional prevailing religion, has been severely proscribed. For nearly thirty years agriculture has been collectivized and nomadism eliminated. And in recent years, the Kazakh herdsmen have been pushed further out of their patrimony with the ploughing of millions of acres of "virgin and idle" lands throughout northern Kazakhstan and the resettlement there of several hundred thousand Russians and Ukrainians.

THE FAR EASTERN SECTOR

The Sino-Soviet boundary in the Far East has a uniformity and effectiveness that is not to be found in Inner Asia. For almost its entire length (aproximately 2000 miles), from the uplands of Trans-Baikalia to the Pacific Coast southwest of Vladivostok, it is a physical boundary: it consists of the Amur River and its tributaries, the Argun and Ussuri.

The Far Eastern sector of the Sino-Soviet borderlands may be said to begin near the middle course of the Argun River, a short distance east of Manchouli, where the Chinese Eastern Railway crosses from Siberia into China or into the contemporary Inner Mongolian Autonomous Region. The construction and subsequent history of the railway (see p. 46) demonstrate the exposed position of the Russian Trans-Ussuri territory. Above all, it suggests that the natural hinterland of Vladivostok, the "fortress of the east," is not the Amur valley to the north, but the lands to the northwest, i.e., the provinces of Manchuria and the Inner Mongolian Autonomous Region.

An examination of Soviet and Chinese maps of the area reveals minor cartographic discrepancies, involving perhaps little more than 250 square miles of territory. Soviet maps show the boundary line a short distance to the north of Manchouli and along the southerly channel of the Argun, whereas the Chinese maps put the line somewhat further to the north.

Nevertheless, by treaty, the Argun constitutes the boundary between Eastern Siberia (Chita Oblast) and the Inner Mongolian Autonomous Region for at least 600 miles. Downstream, the union of the Argun and the Shilka, which enters from the Trans-Baikal mountains on the left, creates the Amur River proper. The Amur forms the boundary for the next thousand miles. Thus far, i.e., from the middle Argun to the Amur, the borderlands have consisted of uplands that are rather sparsely settled throughout. To the east, the plateau is terminated by the Great Khingan Mountains. As the Amur flows toward the east and southeast around the hump of the Great Khingan, the elevation of the borderlands decreases, and the landscape begins to reflect the influence of the Pacific. The high parched steppes, characteristic of so much of the Inner Asian and, as we shall see, of the Mongolian sectors, give way imperceptibly to a greener, more luxuriant vegetation as a result of the heavier summer precipitation.

As the Amur continues its southeasterly course, the right, or Chinese, bank remains higher in elevation than the Soviet bank. Low 3000 foot rounded peaks forming the Little Khingan extend eastward almost as far as the Sungari River and effectively separate the Amur valley from the fertile Manchurian plain to the south. However, on the Soviet side, near the mouth of the Zeya River, which drains the rugged mountain ranges of eastern Amur Oblast, the uplands recede to the north leaving a wide plain. The Zeya Plain, or Zeya-Bureya Plain, fertile, dotted with collective farms, and comparatively well settled serves as an important local granary. In a region where highlands predominate, the importance of the Zeya-Bureya Plain should not be underestimated. Blagoveshchensk, the administrative center of Amur Oblast and the major city of the plain, has a population of about 95,000. It is situated on the Amur but linked by a branch line to the Trans-Siberian Railway, which runs along higher ground at some distance back from the river.

Toward the southeast the plain narrows and, below its confluence with the Bureya, the Amur is confined by highlands on both sides. Here the Little Khingan Mountains, which parallel the Amur on the Chinese side, are met by the Bureya Range (6500 feet), which extends toward the Amur from the northeast. For a short distance the course of the river is through a narrow gorge with sheer cliffs, a veritable Amur "Iron Gate." Beyond the Bureya and the Little Khingan, the Amur, swollen by the successive addition of the waters of both the Sungari and the Ussuri, flows across an extensive level plain. Bogs and reed thickets are common along the river banks, and even land back from the river is poorly drained. Cultivation occurs mainly in areas of higher elevation and better natural drainage or where drainage has been improved.

East of the Bureya Range the borderland territory on the Soviet side falls within Khabarovsk Krai or, more specifically, between the

Bureya and the mouth of the Ussuri, the Jewish Autonomous Oblast, a subordinate unit within the Krai. The Soviet attempt in the 1930's to create a Jewish homeland in the Far East, known as Birobidzhan, to counteract the appeal of Zionism, was a dismal failure. While the oblast's present population is about 163,000, the Jewish element remains relatively small.

On the Chinese side, from the Little Khingan to the Ussuri, the land is also poorly drained, especially along the lower Sungari. Chinese settlement is sparse. In recent years, however, more Chinese have been taking up land near the Amur and have been making improvements. To the south, in the Manchurian plain, the density of population swells dramatically. Over forty million acres of Manchuria's fertile black soil have already been brought into cultivation, and substantially more may be ploughed. Throughout the plain densities reach 400 persons per square mile. Harbin, where the Chinese Eastern Railway crosses the Sungari, has a population over 1.2 million. Several hundred miles to the south is Mukden, with 2 million, and the port of Dairen, with 1.2 million. The Southern Manchurian industrial region is the largest in China. Moreover, beyond the Great Wall to the southwest lies the densely settled North China Plain.

At the confluence of the Amur and Ussuri Rivers, the Sino-Soviet boundary abruptly changes direction. Having served effectively its international role, the Amur turns and flows northeastward into the Pacific—past Khabarovsk, the chief Soviet city of the Far East, with a population of 330,000, and Komsomolsk, the steel city, with 177,000 inhabitants.

About twenty-five miles above Khabarovsk and the principal mouth of the Ussuri, the Amur is joined by the Kazakevicheva, a branch of the Ussuri. Between the Kazakevicheva and the main course of the Ussuri lie low, flat, uninhabited islands, which Chinese Communist maps include within the People's Republic. On Soviet maps, the boundary follows the Kazakevicheva to the Ussuri proper, and thence south along the Ussuri across marshy lowlands. From the Ussuri, the boundary reaches Lake Khanka via the Sungacha. It then crosses the northern part of the shallow lake and turns to the southwest through a series of low ranges where, inland from the coast, it terminates. From that point to the Pacific, the USSR shares a common frontier with the Korean People's Republic.

East of the Ussuri, in the Maritime Krai, the terrain rises into the low, heavily wooded, Sikhote-Alin. The range parallels the coast from north of the port city of Vladivostok to the mouth of the Amur, effectively cutting off the valley from the Pacific. The most concentrated Soviet settlement in Maritime Krai occurs in the Lake Khanka Plain and in and about Vladivostok, which has a population of 283,-000. Along the coast there are scattered fishing villages and, it is reported, numerous naval and military installations. To the west of the Ussuri, in Manchuria, the Nadan Khada-Alin projects northward to separate the Ussuri and Lake Khanka Plains from the lower Sungari. The range is a continuation of the Eastern Manchurian Highlands that extend through the Sino-Soviet-Korean boundary zone.

In the middle of the 19th century, when the Russians took possession of the Amur, the lands on either side were inhabited by primitive tribes. These included Palaeo-Asiatics, such as the Nivkhi (Gilyaks), as well as Manchus and other groups belonging to the Tungus-Manchurian family. They lived by hunting, trapping, and fishing. To the west, in and beyond the Great Khingan, were various groups of Mongol pastoralists. The Russian advance into the Far East quickened the pace of Chinese settlement in Manchuria, while the Trans-Siberian Railway facilitated Russian occupance from the west. Thus, today, with the exception of the Mongols in the Khingan region, the minority groups are of little significance. Even the Mongols total little more than 350,000, while the Manchus, numbering over 2 million have adopted the Chinese language.

The development of the Eastern Siberian and Far Eastern borderlands, however, pales alongside that of Manchuria (see Table II). The Manchurian plain contains 7 per cent of China's 600 million inhabitants. The railways, part of which were built originally by the Russians, have facilitated movement and industrial development. While the resource base of the territory is not especially rich, it was extensively developed in the south—mainly by the Japanese in the

Table II   *Population of Chinese Borderlands*
(1957 estimate)

Manchuria	
Heilungkiang	14,860,000
Kirin	12,550,000
Liaoning	24,090,000
Inner Mongolia AR	9,200,000
Sinkiang-Uighur AR	5,640,000
Total	66,340,000

Source: *Encyclopaedia Britannica World Atlas,* Chicago, 1961, p. 153.

1930's. Accordingly, Southern Manchuria, often called the "Ruhr of the Far East," has a broadly diversified manufacturing base, producing thirty per cent of China's coal, at least seventy per cent of its iron, and half of its electric power.

In contrast, the Soviet population of the Far Eastern borderlands probably totals little more than four million. Of those, more than half are urbanized. Thus the countryside is sparsely occupied and has a rough appearance. Cropland amounts to little more than five million acres. Between 1954 and 1956, about a million acres of virgin and unused land were ploughed, but one cannot assume that this area is altogether suitable for crops. A short growing season, poorly-drained soils, and permafrost have been effective to date in restricting the agricultural potential. In effect, therefore, the Soviet Far Eastern population clings to the Trans-Siberian Railway, on which it heavily depends; a short distance to the north, for many hundreds of miles stretch almost impassable mountains. Furthermore, a rather weak industrial resource base operates against the efforts of the Soviet regime to quicken development. Low quality iron ores have prevented the construction of a fully-integrated iron and steel mill at Komsomolsk. Although coal is found in quantity, its quality is of a medium grade for coking purposes. Sakhalin produces ten per cent of Soviet oil, but its fields are the only significant producers in Siberia east of the Urals and output is insufficient to meet the needs of both industry and the military. On the other hand, the water resources of the Amur basin, as well as the overall forest wealth, are considerable, although relatively little exploitation of either has occurred to date.

THE MONGOLIAN SECTOR

Whereas in the Inner Asian and Far Eastern sectors of the border-lands Sino-Soviet contact occurs along a common international boundary, this is not so in the intervening Mongolian sector. Here the Mongolian People's Republic, or Outer Mongolia, lies between the two states, preventing contiguity (Map, p. 2). Today, therefore, Russians and Chinese come in contact over a wide stretch of Mongolian territory, a zone rather than a line, which has been recognized by both the USSR and the CPR as having independent status (see Table III).

Table III *Population, by Ethnic Groups, of the Mongolian People's Republic*
(1956)

Khalkha Mongols	639,100
Other Mongols	119,300
Kazakhs	36,700
Chinese	16,200
Russians	13,400
Others	20,800
Total	845,500

Source: *Encyclopaedia Britannica World Atlas,* Chicago, 1961, p. 175.

Until very recently we might have selected the southern boundary of the MPR as the *de facto* boundary between the USSR and the CPR. From 1921 until 1955 the MPR was little more than a satellite of the USSR, and all former Chinese influence was excluded. In-deed, according to Professor N. N. Poppe, who left the Soviet Union during World War II, there were plans under discussion in the USSR prior to 1941 to annex the MPR, incorporating it probably into the adjacent Soviet Buriat (Mongol) ASSR.

The Communist success and the subsequent emergence of a strongly organized state in China have not escaped the notice of the Mongols. Though trained in and politically oriented toward Mos-cow, the present Mongol leaders are aware of their unique geo-graphic position. Complete independence could never be realizable for land-locked Outer Mongolia, but the republic does stand to gain from both the USSR and the CPR if peace and stability are maintained. For this reason the Mongols, obviously with the acquiescence of the Soviets, have been willing and able to accept economic aid and assistance from Peking. Currently, a revolution is altering the traditional face of the land. Ulan-Bator, the capital, with a population of 120,000 in a land holding scarcely a million, is taking on the shape of a modern city, as this writer personally discovered in the late summer of 1959. The traditional felt yurt is giving way to the apartment house. Elsewhere, bridges and roads are being constructed and irrigation works are being installed. Much, if not all, of this improvement is being undertaken by Chinese labor sent in from the CPR. After a five-year contract period, the Chinese may either accept Mongol citizenship and settle in the republic, or they may return to China. Some estimates suggest that up to 60,000 Chinese are at work in Mongolia; they live and work apart from the Mongols.

Outer Mongolia is essentially a dry plateau extending 1470 miles from east to west and 780 miles from north to south (Map, p. 4). It rises from an elevation of about 4000 feet in the southeast, bordering Inner Mongolia (China) to 5500 feet in the center. Much of the southern half of the country lies within the Gobi Desert, a flat wasteland. Toward the north and west, mountains such as the Khangai and the Mongolian Altai rise above the level of the plateau, the latter reaching elevations of up to 15,000 feet. Extensive grasslands cover the rest of the republic and contribute substantially to its economy. The pastures can support millions of head of livestock, including cattle, yaks, sheep, and goats, as well as horses and camels. Through the years of the republic's history, the livestock and livestock products have been marketed in the USSR. Because of aridity, crop cultivation is restricted primarily to the north along the Selenga River. In recent years, however, virgin lands in the central part of the republic, west of Ulan Bator, have been ploughed for wheat and corn with varying degrees of success. Near Karakorum, site of Genghis Khan's 13th century capital, the waters of the Orkhon, a tributary of the Selenga, are being used to irrigate the land.

According to Owen Lattimore, the 2700-mile long Sino-Mongolian boundary that separates Outer Mongolia from Inner Mongolia, an integral part of China, reflects a basic cleavage between the two areas which goes back to fundamental factors of geography and tribal history. The Mongols of Inner Mongolia, nearer to and thus more closely associated for many centuries with the intensive cultivators of the North China Plain, have developed a markedly different character from that of the traditional nomads of the outer territory. Moreover, slightly more moist conditions than prevail in and north of the Gobi have made dry farming more successful. While there are more Mongols in Inner Mongolia than in Outer Mongolia, Chinese migration and settlement in the former region have proceeded to such an extent since 1900 that today the Chinese greatly outnumber the Inner Mongols. In spite of this, the Chinese Communists, in accordance with their nationality policy modeled on that of the USSR, which preserves the form if not the substance of the minority national culture, have preserved Inner Mongolia as the Inner Mongolian Autonomous Region.

A careful study of Soviet and Chinese Communist maps of the Sino Mongolian boundary reveals a number of discrepancies, not all of which have obvious geographic significance. On Soviet maps, the international boundary in the west is drawn along the crest of the Mongolian Altai southeastward from the Soviet frontier, but Chinese maps show the boundary considerably to the east. In effect, Chinese maps have incorporated the Mongolian Altai into Sinkiang, thus securing control of the upper waters of a number of the local rivers and the oases to the west. Other variations in the Sino-Mongolian boundary occur through the sparsely occupied Gobi to the east as well as in the plateau region near the Siberian frontier (west of the Argun). Most of these discrepancies are also to the disadvantage of the MPR.

While the different interpretations of the location of the Sino-Mongolian boundary raise the possibility of conflict in the traditional sense, the Soviet-Mongolian boundary shows no discrepancy. Much of it was determined by a treaty between Russia and China dating from the early 18th century. The only recent modification occurred in 1944 when the Soviet leaders annexed Urianghai, or Tannu-Tuva, which they had detached from Outer Mongolia two decades before and set up nominally as an independent republic. Tannu-Tuva was renamed the Tuvinian Autonomous Oblast and made directly subordinate to Moscow. The Tuvinians are a Turkic people.

For the most part, the Soviet-Mongolian boundary cuts across territory that, because of its difficult terrain, is sparsely occupied. From the Altai Mountains in the west to the plateau and ranges of Trans-Baikalia, the borderlands consist of one mountain mass after another, heavily wooded on the north face but dry and bare on the south.

Known as the Alps of Siberia, the Altai Mountains rise to about 10,000 feet. Because of their latitude, they receive fairly heavy precipitation throughout the year. Faulted and deeply dissected, the Altai have a rugged appearance, the grandeur of which is accentuated by the snow, which remains all year round on the higher peaks. In the Altai near the Mongolian border rise several of the headwater tributaries of the Ob, such as the Chuya, the Kamun, and the Biya.

Eastward the Altai give way to the Sayan system, which from the air looks more like a deeply dissected plateau than a series of mountain ranges. The Soviet incorporation of Tannu-Tuva, an enclosed upland basin, placed the boundary to the south of the Tannu-Ola Range. This act resulted in a considerable shortening of the boundary and at the same time gave the USSR a natural advantage. Tannu-Tuva lies astride the shortest and easiest route between western Siberia and Mongolia.

To the east, the Soviet-Mongolian boundary stretches across the ranges of the Eastern Sayan, which are higher than those of the Western Sayan. North of Lake Khobso Gol, the largest fresh-water lake in Mongolia, the boundary descends into a broad upland valley, which facilitates contact between north-central Mongolia and Irkutsk, the major city in eastern Siberia. Eastward, the Dzhedinsk Range forms much of the boundary as far as the Selenga "crossing." The Selenga, the major river of Mongolia, drains northward into Lake Baikal, creating a natural route between the two countries. Not only does a motor road follow the valley, but a railway also enters Mongolia from the north connecting Ulan-Ude on the Trans-

Siberian to Ulan-Bator, the capital of the MPR and, ultimately, to Peking. The Mongolian Railway, opened in its entirety in 1956, thus affords the most direct rail link between Moscow and the Chinese capital.

East of the Selenga, the boundary rises into and crosses a series of relatively low ranges. To the east of the Onon River, the mountains give way to an extensive undulating plateau. Here, the boundaries of the USSR, the MPR, and the CPR meet. The shortest distance between Lake Baikal and Vladivostok on the Pacific is due east across Inner Mongolia and Manchuria, but the Sino-Soviet boundary, as we have already seen, follows the Argun northward to the Amur and around the hump of the Great Khingan.

In the Soviet territories immediately bordering Mongolia on the north, from Altai Krai to Chita Oblast, live approximately 12 million people (Table IV). Of these, some 500,000 belong to non-Slavic ethnic groups. In the Baikal area, mainly east of the lake,

Table IV *Population of the Siberian and Soviet Far Eastern Borderlands* (*1959*)

I. Soviet Far East	4,347,000
of which	
Khabarovsk Krai	1,142,000
(Jewish A.O.	163,000)
Amur Oblast	718,000
Maritime Krai	1,381,000
II. Eastern Siberia	6,960,000
of which	
Krasnoyarsk Krai	2,615,000
(Khakass A.O.	411,000)
Tuva A.O.	172,000
Irkutsk Oblast	1,976,000
(Ust-Orda Buriat N.O.	147,000)
Buriat A.S.S.R.	673,000
Chita Oblast	1,036,000
III. Western Siberia	11,252,000
of which	
Altai Krai	2,683,000
(Gorno-Altai A.O.	157,000)
Kemerovo Oblast	2,786,000

Source: *Narodnoe khoziaistvo RSFSR v 1959 godu. Statisticheskii ezhegodnik,* Moscow, 1960, pp. 36-37.

live approximately 250,000 Buriat Mongols. In the Tuvinian A.O., reorganized in October, 1961 as the Tuva ASSR, are close to 100,000 Tuvinians. To the west and north are other smaller Turkic-speaking groups, such as the Khakass (56,000) and the Altais (45,000). The rest of the population is essentially Russian, mixed with Ukrainian.

During the Soviet period, the Siberian borderlands have undergone impressive industrialization. Between the Salair Range and the Kuznetsk Ala-Tau lies the Kuznetsk Basin, containing the largest deposits of high-quality coal in the USSR. Today the basin has seven cities, each with a population of over 100,000, the largest being Stalinsk (now Novokuznetsk), the steel city (377,000). Beyond the basin to the northwest lies the "primate city" of Siberia, Novosibirsk, with about 900,000 inhabitants. An administrative, industrial and transportation city, Novosibirsk is destined to become also the center of Soviet science in Siberia. Krasnoyarsk on the Yenisei has grown to over 400,000, while Irkutsk on the Angara is not far behind with 365,000. The hydro developments on the Angara at Irkutsk and Bratsk and greater use of the nearby Chermekhovo coal fields, as planned, should speed up the growth of the Baikal area. During the summer of 1961, the concrete dam at Bratsk, begun in 1955, was completed. When filled, its reservoir, the Soviets claim, will be the largest man-made lake in the world, extending 350 miles upstream and reaching a width of 15 miles. The designed capacity of the new Bratsk hydro-electric station is 4.5 million kilowatts. Meanwhile, the three-century old town of Bratsk has been submerged and the population relocated in a new city of 50,000, 20 miles downstream.

East of Lake Baikal, the population (partly Buriat) spreads out over the plateau, while the industrial cities of Ulan-Ude and Chita are both relatively small (170,000 each). From Novosibirsk to Chita, agriculture is restricted by the short growing season and, in many years, insufficient precipitation. The raising of livestock is the preferred activity of the Mongol and Turkic groups, but crop cultivation is also carried on, with grains predominating.

Yet, in spite of the growth of cities and the development of industry in the borderlands, Siberia remains very much a frontier country. To the north for at least two thousand miles lie the empty lands of the forest and tundra, an ever-present fact of geography that creates enormous problems and challenges.

In the years since the Communists overran China, Peking has steadily consolidated its position along the southern border of the Mongolian People's Republic. This includes the Inner Mongolian Autonomous Region in the east, an extension of the Kansu province northward to the international boundary in the center and, in the far west, the Sinkiang-Uighur Autonomous Region.

Over the past sixty years there has been a gradual but steady movement of Chinese settlers into Inner Mongolia, a movement that was facilitated by the construction of railways. This was particularly true in eastern Inner Mongolia, which was served by the Southern Manchurian and Chinese Eastern railways and interconnecting lines. However, the short line northwestward from Peking, which since 1956 has afforded a direct route to Ulan-Bator, has stimulated Chinese settlement beyond the Great Wall north and west of Kalgan, among the Chahar Mongols. Yet, without irrigation, only extensive agriculture with heavy dependence on livestock is presently feasible over much of Inner Mongolia. This has been the traditional economy of Inner Mongolia, contrasting with the intensive Chinese cultivation south of the Great Wall and with the nomadism of the Outer Mongols north of the Gobi. Industrial development, however, will surely attract more Chinese. Under construction is a full-cycle iron and steel plant at the city of Paotow. There are about 1.2 million Mongols in Inner Mongolia, but they are already outnumbered by Chinese, five to one.

Modern Kansu province, bordering on the MPR to the west of the Inner Mongolian A.R., lies astride the historic route between China proper and the dry reaches of Inner Asia. To the north lie the arid wastes of the Gobi, to the south the towering Nan-Shan. Life along the Kansu corridor is sustained by and centered in oases, traditionally guarded by the Great Wall from the attack of northern nomads. In recent years a railway has been constructed through the corridor from Lanchow westward into Sinkiang that ultimately will connect with the Soviet Turk-Sib. The corridor, therefore, is a strategic one whose importance has been further underlined by the discovery and exploitation of oil at Yumen, where reserves have been estimated at 500 million tons, one of the largest deposits in modern China. Because the corridor has permitted the flow of peoples and cultures from east to west throughout history, its population today is heterogeneous. In addition to Chinese, there are large minorities of Dungans (Chinese Muslims), Mongols (and Kalmyks), Turkic-speaking groups, and Tibetans.

II

The Zone of Tension

IN VIEW of the weakness of the native tribes and peoples of central and northern Asia, a 16th century geopolitician might have come to the conclusion that the two centers of power at either end of the Asian land mass, Muscovy and China, would one day find themselves with common frontiers. By mid-17th century, he would have been confirmed in his prognostication and amazed, too, that so little time had been required for the event to pass. For the expansion of Russia into and across Siberia came with dramatic swiftness. Whatever the obstacles—resistance by this or that tribe, a difficult terrain in an inclement climate—they were quickly surmounted. But the force of that drive was rather abruptly halted when the Russians reached the outer limits of the Chinese realm. They would have to summon from the distant western citadel additional strength of men and supplies before the advance could continue. Moreover, the Russia of the Romanovs had reached the outer limits of the Celestial Empire, however vaguely defined, at a time when China, after a period of decline, had received a new organizational lift from the conquering Manchus.

Ancient China, the Middle Kingdom of the Yellow River Basin, had suffered through cycles of power and decline. In periods of its greatest glory, as during the Han Dynasty, 202 B.C.-A.D. 220, and again during the T'ang Dynasty, A.D. 618-906, the Chinese Empire had reached far out into Asia, including southern Manchuria, Mongolia, Turkestan, Tibet, and Indo-China. Later, during the Mongol period, 1260-1368, China south of the Great Wall was the richest part of the vast Mongol empire, which extended across Asia right into the lands of the Rus. In the centuries that followed, however, China was plagued by internal disorders and attacks by outsiders. Finally, in

1644, invaders from Manchuria captured Peking and established the Manchu or Ch'ing Dynasty, giving China in the latter 17th and early 18th centuries one of its greatest periods in modern history.

From the beginning, the coming together of Russians and Chinese in Asia created tension—a tension that originated in the Amur Basin, quickly spread into the Mongolian plateau and, by the middle of the 19th century, penetrated into Turkestan. While China remained strong, Russia was compelled to go easy. But at the first sign of Manchu weakness, which appeared in the 1840's, and particularly as European imperialism gathered momentum, Russia prepared for a further expansion of her empire at the expense of China. As George Kennan recently pointed out,[1] once established in Asia, Russia was compelled from "sheer geopolitical necessity" to protect from foreign penetration and domination those areas which lie adjacent to Russian borders, namely, Manchuria, Outer Mongolia, and Sinkiang. Nor did Russian interest in the borderlands lessen with the collapse of the Chinese Empire in 1911 and her own revolutions of 1917. While the Soviet leaders made a great point of condemning Tsarist imperialism, they were no less inclined to preserve whatever they could of the Russian position in Asia, in part out of fear of Japan's militarism and in part because the Chinese Nationalists were unable to occupy effectively all of the traditional Chinese territories.

From the middle of the 17th to the middle of the 20th centuries, therefore, the ever-narrowing zone of contact between the Russian and Chinese Empires in Asia was one of tension and at times outright conflict.

SEVENTEENTH AND EIGHTEENTH CENTURIES

The Ural Mountains, the traditional boundary between Europe and Asia, have never constituted a barrier to east-west movement. It was, therefore, only a matter of thirty years after Ivan IV had defeated the Volga remnants of the once powerful Mongol Horde and captured Kazan (1552) and Astrakhan (1556), that Slavic freebooters had crossed into Sibir (Map, p. 29). Theirs was not a private

[1] George F. Kennan, "Stalin and China," *The Atlantic Monthly,* May, 1961, p. 35.

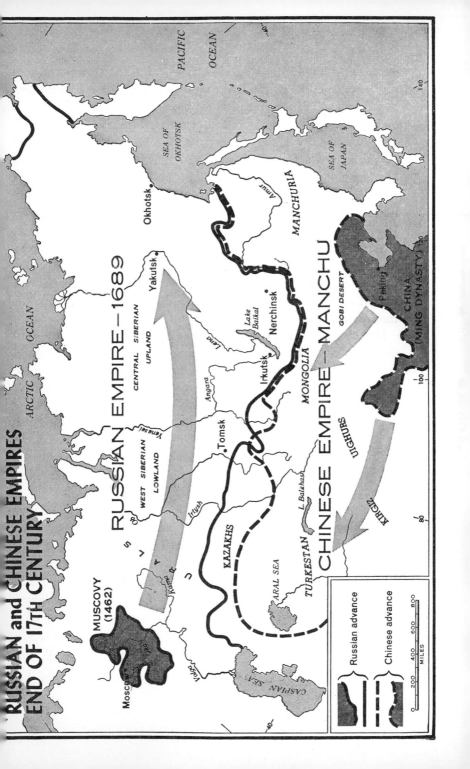

RUSSIAN and CHINESE EMPIRES
END OF 17TH CENTURY

PACIFIC OCEAN

ARCTIC OCEAN

SEA OF OKHOTSK

SEA OF JAPAN

Okhotsk

MANCHURIA

Amur

RUSSIAN EMPIRE – 1689

CENTRAL SIBERIAN UPLAND

Yakutsk

Lake Baikal

Nerchinsk

Lena

Irkutsk

CHINESE EMPIRE – MANCHU

GOBI DESERT

Peking

CHINA (MING DYNASTY)

MONGOLIA

Angara

WEST SIBERIAN LOWLAND

Yenisei

Tomsk

Irtysh

UIGHURS

L. Balkhash

KAZAKHS

TURKESTAN

KIRGIZ

Kama R.

ARAL SEA

MUSCOVY (1462)

Moscow

Volga

CASPIAN SEA

Russian advance

Chinese advance

MILES

0   200   400   600   800

100

140

80

40

60

search for a "final frontier" for Muscovy, which had originated centuries before in the poorly drained, wooded lands of the Volga-Oka "mesopotamia" to the west. Rather, their attraction was the wealth of furs and, perhaps, of precious metals which Siberia possessed.

A half century later, however, after following the rivers and skirmishing with the weakly organized native tribes, the freebooters had established a string of fortified posts across the Vasyugan plain, which was peremptorily annexed to the Russian state by the tsar. In swift succession new posts were built to the east: Kuznetsk, 1618; Yeniseisk, 1619; Krasnoyarsk, 1628; Ilimsk, 1630; and Bratsk, 1631. Keeping well to the north of the open steppe and thereby avoiding contact with the numerous warlike tribes of Turkestan, the Russian drive across Siberia came up against little opposition until it reached Lake Baikal and the land of the Buriat Mongols, the most northerly of the Mongol peoples of East Asia.

Deflected to the north by Mongol resistance, the Russians moved down the upper Lena Valley founding Yakutsk in 1632. Overland the Sea of Okhotsk was reached in 1639. The scattered, primitive tribes of eastern Siberia proved no match for the Russians, and in 1643 Poyarkov crossed the Stanovoi Mountains into the Amur Basin. Following the Zeya River to the Amur, he explored the latter to its mouth before turning northward to the Sea of Okhotsk. In 1651, a post was established at the junction of the Shilka and Argun; four years later, at the junction of the Nercha and the Shilka, Nerchinsk was founded.

The Russian drive was now poised for the conquest of the Amur Basin. However, the expansion into Trans-Baikalia had brought the Russians into contact with Manchus and Chinese, as well as with Mongols. Indeed, five years before the Russians reached the Sea of Okhotsk, the Manchus, with the aid of eastern Mongols, had seized Peking and established the Manchu or Ch'ing Dynasty. These events prompted the Muscovite tsar to send missions to Peking with the hope of establishing diplomatic relations and, above all, to obtain information about the Celestial Empire and its extent and power.

Although China under the Ming Dynasty (1368-1644) had, because of its weakness, been compelled to retreat to within the Great Wall, the Manchus provided a new organizing force and drive which, in the following century, restored the old empire and carried its banners far beyond its previous extent (Map, p. 29). The penetration of the Amur by the Russians, especially after the Buriats were subdued and Irkutsk established in 1661, caused the Manchus to throw open their traditional lands in Manchuria to Chinese settlement.

Up to 1644, the Manchu tribes were said to have carried back to Manchuria over one million peasants during their periodic raids south of the Great Wall on the declining Ming empire. Moreover, Southern Manchuria, particularly the lands along the Liao and Hun Rivers, had been ethnically Chinese since the 3rd century b.c. Now the Manchus were encouraging the Chinese to move north. From 1668 to 1673, however, they reversed their policy and forbade the Chinese to settle beyond Mukden, in the hope of preserving their patrimony intact. Yet from time to time in the later years of the 17th century, a large number of Chinese peasants were smuggled into Manchuria.

After a period of attack and counterattack between Russian and Chinese forces the latter, because of superior strength, were able to halt the Russian drive. By the Treaty of Nerchinsk in 1689, not only were the Russians prevented from navigating the Amur, but the boundary between the Russian and Manchu empires was drawn along the Argun River and the Stanovoi Mountains, far to the north. In the most easterly part, where the mountains turn north, the line was never precisely determined. Although the Manchus surrendered northeastern Siberia to the Russians, the Amur Basin for the next century and a half remained under the Manchus. Peter the Great might cherish the ambition of conquering all of the Far East, right up to the Great Wall, and Catherine might recognize the value of the Amur as a route of supply to her possessions in Kamchatka, but Russian strength in eastern Siberia was relatively too weak to do anything about it.

According to Owen Lattimore, it was the alliance between the Manchus and the neighboring Eastern Mongols, that had made the

Manchu conquest of China possible in 1644. "The Manchu-Mongol alliances," he wrote, "built up a frontier power in Inner Mongolia, which protected the Manchu conquests in China; and it was only later, by using their position in Inner Mongolia as a fulcrum, that the Manchus extended their power into Outer Mongolia." [2] Indeed, it was the greatest of the Manchu emperors, K'ang Hsi (1662-1722), who succeeded in bringing under Chinese control the tribes of northern Manchuria, northern and western Mongolia, Turkestan, and Tibet.

The Russian advance into Baikalia and the establishment of a post at Irkutsk in 1661 created the possibility of serious Russo-Chinese rivalry in Mongolia. The Mongolian plateau possessed a strategic value for the Russians because, across its rolling grasslands, lay one of the most direct routes to Peking. In 1676, Spathary, the leader of a tsarist mission to Peking, reported three possible routes into China from Russian territory. One was through Manchuria, but this route was closed later by the Treaty of Nerchinsk. Another followed the Irtysh River into and through northern Turkestan, but, in addition to being a more circuitous route, it was also hazardous because of the conflicts among the Mongol tribes living there. The third possibility followed the natural corridor of the Selenga River south of Lake Baikal, past the Russian post at Selenginsk, which had been established in 1665. The Selenga valley and its tributaries, the Orkhon and Tola, debauched deep into the plateau, northwest of Peking; but also the Selenga route carried difficulties because of Mongol conflicts.

During the century or more preceding 1676, after the passing of the great Mongol Khans, the Mongol Empire had disintegrated into small independent tribal states. For some time the tribes of northern and western Mongolia had been at war. Possibly because some of the Western Mongols had been on relatively good terms with the Russians in Siberia—indeed, in 1628 some tribes, later known as Kalmyks, had migrated freely to the Volga, where they settled—the Northern Mongols requested the protection of

[2] Owen Lattimore, *The Mongols of Manchuria*, New York: The John Day Company, 1934, p. 16.

the Manchu emperor, which they got in 1691. The Treaty of Kiakhta, signed in 1727 between Russia and China, permitted Russian traders to cross Mongolia. Northern or Outer Mongolia, as well as the lands to the south, or Inner Mongolia, were clearly part of the emperor's domain. The boundary between the Russian and Chinese empires accordingly was drawn through the Sayan Mountains, south and west.

In the early years of dominance, the Ch'ing emperors, who in effect acted as feudal overlords, favored the Outer Mongols, and thereby brought an element of stability to the plateau that it had not known for many generations. Nevertheless, Russian trade with China across Outer Mongolia did not materialize until later. In the period from 1730 to 1850 there were few exchanges between the Russians and the Chinese in Mongolia.

Chinese contacts with the lands and peoples to the west of Mongolia are of ancient vintage. In 139 b.c. the Han emperor sent an envoy to Hsi-yu, or the "western land." After a period of Chinese attack and conquest, virtually all of the western principalities, including Fergana in what is now Uzbekistan, paid tribute to China. Several centuries later, with the emergence of a Western Turkic Confederation, the vassal relationship was broken. However, the link was restored during the 7th century, only to be weakened again in subsequent centuries. Tibetans overran the region, and they were followed by Turkic tribes (Uighurs) migrating from the Mongolian plateau. Muslim Arabs from the west invaded Turkestan in the 10th century, and finally in the 13th century came the Mongol tribes under Genghis Khan.

With the collapse of the Mongol empire, which was followed by tribal conflicts, the Chinese were again able to extend their rule into Turkestan. By 1757, the Ch'ing emperor had smashed the power of the Western Mongols in Dzhungaria and overrun the oases of the Tarim. A new province was created: Dzhungaria and the Tarim Basin (Kashgaria) were united and called Sinkiang, "the new dominion."

In order to strengthen the Chinese defense of the western frontier of Sinkiang, Sibos and other Manchurian tribes were settled along the Ili. In 1760 about 10,000 Uighur families from the Tarim Basin were also settled in the valley. These people later were called Taranchais, or "agriculturalists," because, in contrast to the Kazakh and Mongol tribes, who were nomadic, the Uighurs were sedentary peoples. In 1771 some Kalmyks who had settled along the Volga in the preceding century, returned to their homeland.

In the decades that followed, Chinese control of Sinkiang was exercised mainly through the local chieftains and headmen, who were vassals of the emperor. Chinese policy was clearly one of divide and rule. There was little settlement from the Chinese provinces to the east, for the Chinese did not consider Sinkiang a desirable place to live. In a sense, Sinkiang was to them what Siberia was to the Russians. In 1757 the new dominion had been proclaimed a place of exile for criminals or political dissenters. Hence the only other Chinese in Sinkiang were those attached mainly to military garrisons. They were transported there with their families, given land and seed, and encouraged to make themselves self-sufficient. Yet because the Chinese in Sinkiang were generally always favored by advantageous taxes and other privileges, they were greatly resented by the native peoples.

Various native states west of Sinkiang in Western Turkestan, such as Kokand and Bokhara, and the Kazakh Hordes, submitted to the Ch'ing emperor. However, being so remote from China proper, they were not actually brought under direct control.

The Russians, meanwhile, halted in Mongolia and Manchuria by the strength of the Ch'ing empire, continued active throughout the forests and grasslands of western Siberia, consolidating their hold on the upper reaches of the Yenisei, Ob, and Irtysh Rivers. Omsk, established in 1716, was followed by Semipalatinsk in 1718, and Barnaul in 1738 (maps 4 and 5). In the latter part of the 18th century, the Turkic tribes of the Altai Mountains came under Russian control, and the boundary of Outer Mongolia in the northwest was delimited. But there could be no direct Russo-Chinese exchange in Inner Asia so long as the Russians remained north of the grasslands of the Kazakh nomads. It required almost another century of Russian expansion, this time into the dry plains sur-

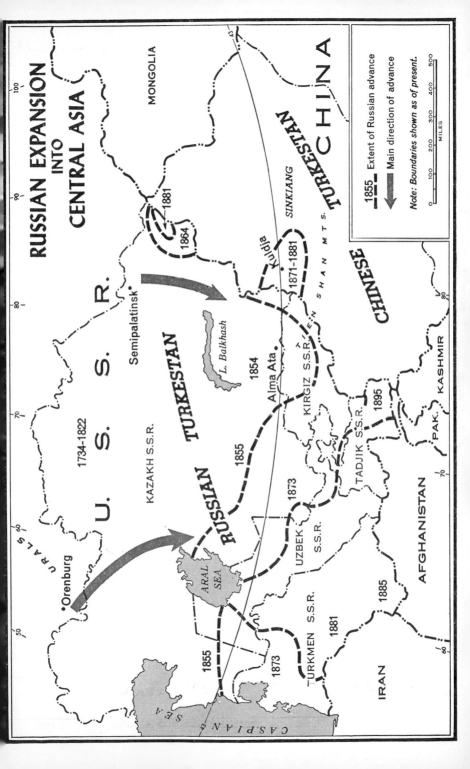

RUSSIAN EXPANSION INTO CENTRAL ASIA

1855 — Extent of Russian advance

➤ Main direction of advance

Note: Boundaries shown as of present.

MILES
0 100 200 300 400 500

MONGOLIA

CHINA

TURKESTAN

SINKIANG

CHINESE

Kuldja

1871-1881

TIEN SHAN MTS.

KASHMIR

PAK.

AFGHANISTAN

IRAN

Semipalatinsk

U. S. S. R.

TURKESTAN

L. Balkhash

1854

Alma Ata.

KIRGIZ S.S.R.

TADJIK S.S.R.

1895

1734-1822

KAZAKH S.S.R.

RUSSIAN

1855

1873

UZBEK
S.S.R.

1885

Orenburg

URALS

ARAL
SEA

1855

1873

TURKMEN S.S.R.

1881

CASPIAN SEA

1864

1881

rounding the Aral Sea, before Russians and Chinese would meet in Turkestan.

NINETEENTH AND EARLY TWENTIETH CENTURIES

The century ending in 1789 marked the high point of China under the Ch'ing Dynasty. Thereafter, the Empire's decline was sharp and perilous.

The tsarist government, aware of the increasing importance of its Pacific settlements, turned again to the problem of the Amur, which had been quiescent since 1689. Following the Opium War (1840-42), which demonstrated Ch'ing weakness, Russian pressure on the Amur again manifested itself. In 1846 an expedition was sent to explore the Amur, and in 1850, in violation of the Treaty of Nerchinsk, a Russian post was established at Nikolayevsk near the mouth. A trans-Baikal army was organized and other posts established, even on Sakhalin Island. The Russian advance, directed locally by the ambitious Nicholas Muraviev, Governor General of Eastern Siberia, took two directions: (a) eastward from Baikal and (b) southward along the coast from Okhotsk and Kamchatka. Unable to resist, the Chinese were compelled to negotiate and to recognize the conquest that the Russians had achieved.

The Treaty of Aigun in 1858 established a new Russo-Chinese boundary along the Amur, from the mouth of the Argun to the Pacific. The territory south of the Amur and east of the Ussuri was placed under joint occupation, and the Russians founded Khabarovsk. Two years later, in the Treaty of Peking, the Russians forced another settlement on the Manchus. Russia took complete control of the territory east of the Ussuri, now known as the Maritime Krai, and Manchuria was further pared down. In the meantime, the Russian Pacific naval base, which had first been established at Petropavlovsk on Kamchatka, and later moved to Nikolayevsk near the mouth of the Amur, was advanced in 1872 to Vladivostok, where the problem of winter ice was less severe.

The apparent collapse of Manchu China encouraged Russian expansion, though essentially of an economic nature, in the Mongolian sector. A convention in 1860 between Russia and China established

Russian trade with Outer Mongolia on an official basis. In the next year a Russian consulate was opened near the Buddhist monastery at Urga, now Ulan Bator, and Russian merchants entered the Chinese dominion.

Far to the west, where the nomadic Kazakh tribes wandered over the steppe all the way from the Volga River to Dzhungaria, owing allegiance and paying tribute to the Ch'ing emperor, the Russian drive into the Inner Asian drylands also got underway. Already, by the end of the 18th century, trade links had been established across Turkestan between Russia and China. Some of this trade was carried on by the Russian inhabitants at Bukhtarma on the Irtysh, and by the natives at Tarbagatai (or Chuguchak) and Kuldja in Sinkiang. Later other Russian centers, such as Semipalatinsk and Petropavlovsk in western Siberia, were involved. And the Russians had the advantage of greater accessibility to Sinkiang than did the Chinese of the Central Provinces to the east. The journey by camel from Semipalatinsk to Tarbagatai and Kuldja took only two months one way. However, from 6 to 12 months were needed to go from China proper to Kuldja. This factor obviously greatly affected Chinese control of the province, as the decades that followed clearly revealed.

In order to protect and expand their interests in Turkestan, the Russians decided on military conquest of the native peoples of the area. They employed a two-pronged offensive (see map 5). One advance lay southward from the Urals to the Syr-Darya and the borders of the Khanates of Khiva and Bokhara. Persistently, the expeditions of the tsar pushed deeper into the lands nominally under the overlordship of the Chinese emperor, moving from one advance position to another, consolidating as they went. By 1854, they had penetrated southeast of Lake Balkhash, which included the lower Ili valley, one of the main routes into Sinkiang. North of Lake Issyk-Kul, in the foothills of the Tien-Shan, the town of Vernyi, now Alma-Ata, was founded. The Kuldja Convention of 1851 gave Russia greater freedom of trade at Kuldja on the upper Ili and at Tarbagatai. Now they were ready to compel the Chinese to come to terms on a boundary between their respective empires, which would above all recognize the Russian conquests.

The Treaty of Peking, signed in 1860, which determined the Ussuri River boundary in the Far East, also began the process of delimiting the boundary in Inner Asia. Four years later, in the Treaty of Tarbagatai, the boundary was drawn to give the Tien-Shan region south of Lake Issyk-Kul to Russia. The Russian steppe province of Semipalatinsk, augmented by the addition of former Chinese territory, was reorganized in 1865 as Turkestan Oblast.

Because of its distance from Peking, a factor referred to above, Sinkiang was a difficult province to control effectively. Indeed, since the Turkic-speaking peoples had not reconciled themselves to Chinese domination, the vast territory was periodically torn by armed uprisings. These revolts, usually very bloody, were aimed at driving the Chinese from Sinkiang and at separating Sinkiang from the Chinese empire. There were insurrections in 1825-26, 1827, 1830, 1857, and finally in 1864. The latest revolt began in Dzhungaria, involving both Turks and Dungans, and soon succeeded in throwing off the Manchu yoke. In this effort, they were assisted by the Chinese garrisons in Sinkiang, which were composed mainly of Dungans.

While this revolt was occurring north of the Tien-Shan, another uprising occurred in the Tarim Basin. The rebels sought the assistance of Yakub Beg, a Kokandian general in Andijan to the west. He marched an army into Sinkiang and occupied the Tarim oases. Moving north, he defeated the leaders of the Dzhungarian revolt and occupied Urumchi. Yakub established a separate state, which received limited support from both Britain and Turkey. Britain was not unwilling to see a buffer state established between the Russian positions in Turkestan and her own empire in India. However, the separate state survived only until 1877 when Yakub Beg was killed.

The revolt in Sinkiang encouraged the Russians to act. In 1871, a Russian military force crossed the frontier and occupied the upper Ili district, including Kuldja (see map 5). At the same time, the Russians attempted to extract from Peking the cession of the valley of the tributary Tekes River, along with strategic passes through the bordering ranges. The Chinese, however, refused to comply with the demands of the Russians. Therefore, the Russians remained at Kuldja until the Chinese, supported by the European powers who had no desire to see a complete collapse of the Ch'ing Empire, were able to muster the strength to overcome the dissident Muslims. The Treaty of St. Petersburg in 1881 reaffirmed possession of the upper Ili in Chinese hands, and the Russians agreed to relinquish their conquest. That the Russian presence was not unwelcomed in the Ili region by at least some of the native population is evidenced by the fact that, when the Russians withdrew, thousands of Dungans and Uighurs followed the tsarist army into Russian territory and settled there. Under the terms of the treaty, the Chinese ceded a small area west of the Holkuts River to Russia, for the purpose of settling the emigrants there. Most of the Dungans settled near the Chinese border, although some went westward to the Fergana valley.

In spite of the success in subduing the Muslims, Chinese control over Sinkiang remained perilously weak in the decades that followed, even though it had been made a regular province of the Empire in 1884.

Thus Russia, after having been defeated in the Crimean War, was on the move all across Asia. With its political power weakening, the Ch'ing Dynasty could offer little opposition. An effective way to prevent the loss of the borderlands to Russia was to make them unquestionably Chinese. In the later decades of the 19th century, therefore, colonization became a vital goal of imperial Chinese state policy.

Hitherto, the Ch'ing emperors had forbidden Chinese settlement in the central and northern part of Manchuria. Between 1750 and 1806, a series of edicts renewed the prohibition, although the policy was somewhat relaxed in 1803. However, the restriction against Chinese migration was difficult to enforce, and it therefore proved ineffective. It was not possible to preserve the Manchus' patrimony. Chinese infiltration continued and, following the cession of the territory beyond the Amur to Russia in 1858-60, began to intensify. In 1860-61, settlers began moving onto the virgin plains north of Harbin and northwest of Kirin. By 1878, there were more than 100,000 Chinese households north of Harbin. In that year, the Manchus gave their official blessing to the Sinification of the territory.

Settlement in Inner and Outer Mongolia was slower to develop, partly because the aridity compelled an adjustment in traditional Chinese agricultural practices. Nevertheless, as the Trans-Siberian Railway cut a swath across Siberia to Lake Baikal, and Russian settlers found their way into Urianghai and Buriatia, the Manchus countered with projects to establish agricultural communities in the river valleys of northern and central Outer Mongolia.

The first plans for a Trans-Siberian Railway had been proposed in 1855, partly to afford an outlet to European Russia for the grain of western Siberia. Moreover, if Russia was to play a dominant role in Asia, a railway linking its far-flung possessions would have to be built. In 1891, work began on the section from Vladivostok to Khabarovsk on the Amur. From 1892-95 construction proceeded eastward from Cheliabinsk in the Urals to Lake Baikal.

The strengthening of the Russian position in Asia, and especially in the Far East, was dictated also out of fear of Japanese intentions. Indeed, though Russia took advantage of the opportunities presented by the waning power of the Ch'ing Dynasty to expand at China's expense, she also realized that China presented a counterpoise to Japan. This was demonstrated in 1895 when, having defeated China in a brief war, Japan imposed a treaty that would have quickened the Ch'ing collapse. In addition to the Pescadores and Formosa, Japan was ready to seize the Liaotung Peninsula in southern Man-churia with the strategic Port Arthur. Only the combined inter-vention of Russia, Germany, and France compelled Japan to modify her demands. After the war, in exchange for loans and guarantees of friendship, Russia secured from China permission to construct a railway that would link Lake Baikal across Manchuria to Vladi-vostok. Such a line would cut 340 miles off an all-Russian route along the Amur. At the same time, the railway would facilitate the spread of Russian economic, military and political influence through-out Manchuria and North China. When the Germans occupied Kiaochow Bay across the Yellow Sea from Liaotung in 1897, Russia obtained mining rights in southern Manchuria, leases to Port Arthur and nearby Dairen, and permission to extend the railway from Harbin to Dairen. Thus, while posing as China's friend, Russia secured what Japan had won by war and had been subsequently deprived of.

The Boxer Rebellion of 1900 reflected Chinese frustration and resentment over the course of events. Immediately, however, Russia brought Manchuria under military control. Chinese and Manchu villagers on the left bank of the Amur near the mouth of the Zea, who had remained under Manchu administration after 1858, were driven out, and the region was annexed. After the rebellion had subsided, Russia was compelled to retreat to the pre-1900 position she held in Manchuria, although the villages were not restored.

In view of the nature of both Russian and Japanese ambitions in China, conflict was probably unavoidable. Japan watched the Russian advance in Manchuria with steadily increasing concern. When, however, Russian interest manifested itself in the guise of lumber concessions along the Yalu River, in northern Korea, which had come largely within the Japanese sphere after 1895, war soon resulted.

Though adopting an aggressive role in the Far East, Russia was nevertheless ill-prepared to follow through successfully the consequences of that policy. Unable to supply its Far Eastern forces and disrupted by revolution, Russia collapsed completely in 1905. Not only did she surrender to Japan the South Manchurian Railway along with Port Arthur and access to the mineral resources of southern Manchuria but also the southern half of Sakhalin. Sakhalin had become Russian by treaty in 1875 which in turn had conceded Japan title to the Kurile Islands to the northeast. Nevertheless, in the détente that followed in 1907 (and ultimately made Russia and Japan allies of the United Kingdom and France in World War I), Russia and Japan agreed on separate spheres of influence in China. Although Chinese sovereignty over Manchuria was affirmed, Russia recognized Japan's pre-eminent position in the south, and in Inner Mongolia to the east. In return, Russian influence was recognized as paramount in northern Manchuria, Outer Mongolia, and Sinkiang. In effect, therefore, the Russian sphere contained practically all of the territory north of what later came to be called the Kuropatkin Line. Named after General Kuropatkin, the line was drawn along the 43rd parallel, eastward from the Khan-Tengri Range in the Tien-Shan to Vladivostok, bv political strategists in St. Petersburg as a possible boundary between Russia and China in Asia.

The Sino-Japanese War and the Russo-Japanese War, which were fought over Chinese territory, made colonization even more urgent from the Chinese point of view. In 1908, Chinese administration was imposed on Manchuria, and all legal bans on settlement were lifted. Ironically, the Russian-built railways facilitated the Chinese peasant movement northward. The population of Manchuria quickly rose to about 16 million, with somewhat less than seven million in the northern part.

After the turn of the century, Chinese peasant migration into eastern Inner Mongolia also increased, while large-scale systematic colonization began in Outer Mongolia. In 1908, Peking reinforced its garrison in Urga, and began intensive colonization along the Kalgan-Urga caravan route through the Gobi. In 1911, the year the Ch'ing Dynasty was overthrown, a Chinese colonization bureau was opened in Urga to expedite the movement northward. The increasing presence of the Chinese peasant farmer in Mongolia did much to fire Mongol nationalism, already provoked by Chinese economic exploitation and the shrewd Chinese merchants. These developments did not go unnoticed in St. Petersburg. "The reforms planned by China in Mongolia—Chinese tillers to colonize the strips of land bordering us, the linking of the same by railways, at points which would be close to this frontier, with Chinese administrative centers and the distribution of Chinese troops, especially the appearance of considerable Chinese armed forces in the close neighborhood of our possessions, cannot fail to disturb us," it was stated at a conference on foreign affairs in St. Petersburg in 1911. "Therefore, the Mongolian question is for us of great importance, and our support of the Mongols in their aspiration to counteract the above-mentioned undertaking of the Chinese government would fully correspond with our interests." [3]

Early in 1911, the Outer Mongols petitioned the Russian tsar for

[3] Peter S. H. Tang, *Russian and Soviet Policy in Manchuria and Outer Mongolia, 1911-1931,* Durham: Duke University Press, 1959, p. 297.

aid in throwing off the Chinese yoke. The Russians supplied arms and promised assistance, while the collapse of the Ch'ing Dynasty in Peking created the opportunity for intervention.

The revolution in Peking and the establishment of a Chinese Republic made evident at once, according to Owen Lattimore, the old cleavages between Outer and Inner Mongolia. Revolutionary movements had actually begun earlier in Inner Mongolia than in Outer Mongolia, but had never made much headway. Proximity to the North China Plain had given the economy of the Inner Mongols quite a different character from that of their nomadic cousins north of the Gobi; Chinese colonization further enhanced this difference. Among Outer Mongols, however, anti-Ch'ing sentiment was widespread.

Late in 1911, Outer Mongolia proclaimed its independence, but such a development was not desired by Russia. In 1913, therefore, Russia, serving as mediator, forced the Mongols to recognize Chinese suzerainty. Two years later, the future role of Outer Mongolia became clearer, when, in the Kiakhta Agreement, the province was made a buffer between Russia and China. Outer Mongolian autonomy within the Chinese Empire was reaffirmed, but Russia secured the right of free trade in the territory. What this meant in effect was that, despite Chinese suzerainty, Outer Mongolia had become a Russian protectorate. But not for long. Following the revolutionary upheaval in Russia, the President of China, in November, 1919, proclaimed the cancellation of Outer Mongolian autonomy, and Chinese troops crossed the Gobi.

Republican China, however, was no more welcome in Outer Mongolia than Imperial China had been in its later years. In 1918 a People's Revolutionary Party had been formed in Mongolia, and in March, 1921, a provisional government had been proclaimed at Kiakhta, on Russian territory. Several months later, Red Army troops from Lake Baikal entered Urga.

While attempting to gain control of Outer Mongolia as a whole, tsarist Russia occupied and detached the northwestern province from Outer Mongolia. Russian forces had entered Urianghai in 1911. In 1914, a Russian protectorate was proclaimed over it. But with the revolution in Russia, Urianghai again came under Mongol or Chinese jurisdiction, only to have Soviet authority established in 1918. In 1921, Urianghai "proclaimed" itself an independent republic called Tannu-Tuva, but it was clearly a Soviet satellite.

In Sinkiang, to the west, the Russian penetration after 1881 was largely of an economic nature. Following the annexation of the borderlands, especially east of Lake Balkhash in the Semirechie, Cossack settlements had been established. Imposed on the fertile grasslands of the Kazakh nomads, these settlements involved from 12,000 to 15,000 people. Followed soon after by Russian peasant colonization, the inroads of the crop cultivator were sorely resented by the pastoralist. Nevertheless, as far as the tsarist government was concerned, Semirechie faced the most dangerous spot for Russia in Asia. Here were the corridors of Inner Asia. These settlements, therefore, were designed to secure the Russian position against the nomad and afford at the same time a buffer on the Chinese flank.

Decades later, in the middle of World War I, the corridors continued to have an effect on geopolitical thinking in Russia. Indeed, as far as General A. N. Kuropatkin, who became Governor General of Turkestan in 1916, was concerned, ". . . the future danger for Russia from this empire of 400,000,000 people is beyond all doubt. The most vulnerable part of the Russian frontier, as 800 years ago, remains that great gateway through which the hordes of Genghis Khan poured into Europe. So long as Kuldja (i.e., on the Ili) rests in the hands of the Chinese, the protection of Turkestan from China will remain very difficult, or will demand a great number of troops. This gateway must not be left in the hands of the Chinese. A change in our boundary with China is urgently necessary." [4] Thus, Kuropatkin would adopt a boundary that gave Russia all of mainland Asia north of the 43rd parallel—including Kuldja!

The Semirechie settlements enjoyed considerable success. In 1912, the tsarist government granted a charter for a railway to a Semirechie company to further the economic development of the

---

[4] Richard A. Pierce, *Russian Central Asia, 1867-1917,* Berkeley and Los Angeles: University of California Press, 1960, p. 298.

area and to facilitate further colonization. In 1911, the construction of a railway south from Novosibirsk on the Trans-Siberian had begun, but the road reached only Semipalatinsk when the first World War broke out.

The resentment of the Kazakh nomads, the fact that their best grasslands had been occupied and their nomad routes of migration from summer to winter pastures had been cut, led to bloody uprisings against the Russians in mid-summer 1916. It was the seriousness of the situation that led to the appointment of Kuropatkin as governor general. Some Kazakhs continued to fight on against the Imperial Russians; others joined the Bolsheviks, hoping that the success of the latter would benefit their own cause. At any rate, the Bolshevik Revolution of 1917 would have repercussions on all the native peoples of Russian Turkestan.

1917-1945

In the period immediately following the Bolshevik Revolution, the Soviet leaders were inclined to disassociate themselves from tsarist imperial policies. In particular they denounced the treaties that had been imposed on China and condemned tsarist hegemony in the borderlands. Pledges were made to the future equality of Sino-Soviet relationships. Moreover, shortly after the seizure of power, the Soviet leaders promised to transfer to republican China the Chinese Eastern Railway which had been built by Russia and maintained as a Russian state possession.

The collapse of civil government in Russia, however, encouraged the Japanese to intervene on the mainland. On April 5, 1918, Japanese troops landed at and occupied Vladivostok, on the pretext of protecting Japanese lives and property. They thereupon seized the Chinese Eastern Railway and advanced along the Trans-Siberian as far as Chita. In the meantime, Czech troops, which had been captured by the Russians during the World War, began moving eastward along the Trans-Siberian toward their destination, the port of Vladivostok. There they hoped to be removed by the Allies and transported to the western front against Germany. By June, 1918, the anti-Communist Czechs had sealed off western Siberia from Mos-

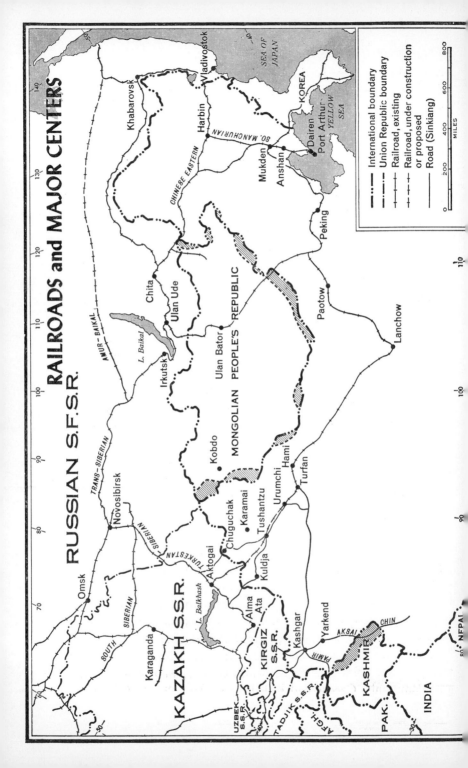

RAILROADS and MAJOR CENTERS

RUSSIAN S.F.S.R.

Legend:
- International boundary
- Union Republic boundary
- Railroad, existing
- Railroad, under construction or proposed
- Road (Sinkiang)

MILES
0   200   400   600   800

SEA OF JAPAN

Khabarovsk

Vladivostok

KOREA

YELLOW SEA

Dairen
Port Arthur

Harbin

CHINESE EASTERN

SO. MANCHURIAN

Mukden

Anshan

Peking

Paotow

Lanchow

Chita

Ulan Ude

L. Baikal

Irkutsk

AMUR-BAIKAL

TRANS-SIBERIAN

Ulan Bator

Kobdo

MONGOLIAN PEOPLE'S REPUBLIC

Novosibirsk

Hami

Urumchi

Turfan

Karamai

Tushantzu

Chuguchak

TURKESTAN SIBERIAN

Aktogai

Kuldja

SIBERIAN

L. Balkhash

Omsk

KAZAKH S.S.R.

Alma Ata

KIRGIZ S.S.R.

Kashgar

Yarkend

AKSAI CHIN

PAMIR

KASHMIR

Karaganda

SOUTH SIBERIAN

UZBEK S.S.R.

TADJIK S.S.R.

AFGH.

PAK.

INDIA

NEPAL

cow. Various anti-Communist Russian "governments" were established from time to time across the vast stretch of Siberia, but it proved impossible to create a single anti-Bolshevik authority to coordinate or unite their activities.

Throughout 1919, the situation gradually worsened for the Bolshevik opposition in Siberia. The Czech legion was finally evacuated, leaving the Bolshevik forces advancing from the west, while the Japanese troops east of Lake Baikal remained the only effective force in Siberia. Under these circumstances, an attempt was made, with Japanese encouragement, to establish a buffer state in eastern Siberia. The Far East Republic, which came into existence in April, 1920, was a compromise. It was neither Bolshevik nor reactionary, but proclaimed itself "independent democratic." In May, the Soviet government recognized it.

Since the Far East Republic had pledged itself not to admit Soviet Russian armies to its territory, the Japanese withdrew their troops to the maritime region. But, by skilful diplomacy, Japan was outmaneuvered. The republic did not take on the characteristics of a buffer. Finally, primarily as a result of pressure from the English-speaking powers, Japan was compelled to withdraw entirely from the mainland. By November, 1922, her troops were back in Japan; the maritime region was incorporated into the Far East Republic; and on November 10, 1922, the republic voted itself into the Russian Soviet Federated Socialist Republic, and ceased to exist as a separate entity. Within the year, a Buriat-Mongol ASSR was established on the shores of Lake Baikal, to accommodate the Mongols of eastern Siberia.

Thus, by 1923, Soviet authority was established throughout Siberia. The withdrawal of the Japanese also gave the Russians possession once again of the Chinese Eastern Railway. But the Soviets did not redeem the promise that they had made earlier, to return the railway to China—primarily because of their fear of and concern over Japanese Far Eastern ambitions. When the Soviets were finally compelled to sell the railway, it was not to China—but to Japan! And the transfer (in 1935) was little more than a recognition of a changed power situation, for in 1931, Japan had invaded Manchuria and sub-sequently established the puppet state of Manchukuo.

In a treaty with China in 1915, Japan had secured 99-year leases over Port Arthur and Dairen, as well as over the South Manchurian Railway. In the years that followed, Japan increasingly dominated the economic life of Manchuria, while leaving the local administra-tion in the hands of Chinese separatist leaders. In the latter 1920's, conflicts between the separatists in Manchuria and the Chinese Kuomintang (or Chinese Nationalists) brought increased tension. Finally, in order to prevent the Chinese Nationalists from gaining control of Manchuria, the Japanese decided to take over the entire province. In the years that followed, from 1933 to 1945, Japan imple-mented the program of development that resulted in the creation of the southern Manchurian industrial base, the so-called "Far Eastern Ruhr."

Soviet strength throughout the period, from the revolution to the second World War, was not sufficient to attempt to dislodge the Jap-anese from their position of paramountcy in Manchukuo and North China, however ardently the Russians might have desired it. At any rate, the Soviet Far Eastern territories had to be strengthened and protected, if possible, without resort to armed conflict. This task was made all the more urgent during the middle and late 1930's as Nazi Germany's militarism posed a threat in Europe to the western bor-derlands of the Soviet Union. Consequently, the Soviet regime de-cided to construct a second Siberian railway which would parallel the main route, but run at some distance to the north of the Mongolian-Manchurian border. Known as the Baikal-Amur Railway, it was planned to link Taishet on the Trans-Siberian northwest of Irkutsk with the new port of Sovetskaya Gavan on the Pacific, almost due east of Komsomolsk. Although construction got underway before World War II only short sections of the railway were completed by 1941, contributing little if anything to Soviet defenses in the Far East. After the war, it was reported that Japanese prisoners of war were put to work on the railway, but there are no known reliable data to indicate that the Baikal-Amur was ever finished.

The autonomous position of Outer Mongolia within the Chinese Empire had been agreed upon by Russia, China and Outer Mongolia in 1915. Real power in Outer Mongolia, however, lay with the Russians—at least until 1917. For a brief period following the Bolshevik Revolution it seemed that Russia would not regain her hegemony over Outer Mongolia. On the other hand, the short-lived rule of Chinese and White Russians in Outer Mongolia revealed how easily the territory might serve as a springboard for attack on the vital Trans-Siberian Railway. Furthermore, Outer Mongolia in any other hands but Soviet Russian might prove a source of disaffection for the Buriat Mongols to the north. In 1921, therefore, the Red Army occupied Urga and in 1924, the Mongolian constitution, modeled on that of the USSR, proclaimed the Mongolian People's Republic. In effect the territory became a Soviet satellite, even though the Russians claimed to recognize—on paper at least— Chinese suzerainty over Outer Mongolia. These developments did not occur without strong protests from China, but there was little that the Chinese Republic could do. For nearly thirty years thereafter the Soviet hold on the Mongolian republic seemed unshakable. The MPR was cut off and isolated from the rest of the world.

As has been mentioned before, nomadic livestock herding had been the traditional occupation of the Outer Mongols for centuries. Prior to 1921, and particularly before 1911, whatever cultivation of the soil there was—and acreage was not large due, in part, to the severity of the climate—was mostly in the hands of Chinese peasant settlers. The Mongol preferred his way of life and despised those who made a living working the soil. With the exodus of most of the remaining Chinese from Mongolia after the Communist revolution of 1921, the new Mongol regime attempted to settle the nomads. In 1929-30, an effort was made to collectivize the agricultural economy of the country, but the movement ended in complete failure. The hostility of the nomads to surrendering their vast herds led to the slaughtering of large numbers of animals. Others drove their sheep and goats over the border into Inner Mongolia to escape collectivization. Few livestock cooperatives survived.

At the same time, the regime (in the First Mongolian Five Year

Plan introduced in 1930) directed that the sown area be raised to over 240,000 acres. But, this effort, too, failed, and as late as 1940, there were no more than 65,000 acres under cultivation in Mongolia.

These efforts to alter drastically the economy of the country must be visualized against a background of state oppression and international tension. The regime waged a systematic campaign against the Mongol social system. Large numbers of Buddhist monks were purged and most of the monasteries were closed. Some monasteries were completely destroyed, their treasures carried away. A new elite was trained in the image created by Moscow. Hence, as World War II approached, the Soviets were unquestionably concerned about Mongolia. In 1936, a Soviet-Mongolian defensive alliance, aimed at Japan, proclaimed that the USSR would defend the MPR as if it were Soviet territory. Indeed, plans had reportedly been made in Moscow for the annexation of the MPR by the USSR. At any rate, the Soviets possibly realized that a Japanese attack on Mongolia might gain the support of the Mongol people as a whole.

With respect to Tannu-Tuva, neither the Mongolian nor the Tuvinians had sought the separation that the Soviets had imposed on them, but in a gesture of conciliation to the Mongols the Russians transferred Darkhat, a small, sparsely inhabited strip west of Lake Khobso Gol, to the MPR. In 1927, less than a fifth of the population of Tannu-Tuva were Russians. In the decades that followed, as a result of systematic colonization, the complexion of the population changed substantially to the disadvantage of the native Tuvinians. Clearly, the Soviet leaders were intent on keeping Tannu Tuva and the MPR apart. Finally, in October, 1944, Tannu Tuva was secretly annexed to the USSR, an event which the rest of the world did not discover until some months later. Reorganized as the Tuvinian Autonomous Oblast directly subordinate to Moscow, the mountain basin was given a unique status in the Soviet political-administrative hierarchy.

On the eve of World War I, according to Louis Fischer, Russia also seriously intended to annex Dzhungaria or the northern half of Sinkiang province. On the other hand, annexation of the Tarim Basin to the south could only antagonize Great Britain because of the special interest which the Tarim Basin held for British India.[5] The move was forestalled by the war and revolution. At any rate, the chaos in Russia, coupled with the difficulties facing the Kuomintang in China proper, allowed Sinkiang to live for several years as a semi-independent state under its Chinese governor.

Because the Bolsheviks were already threatening to disrupt their traditional nomadic way of life, 100,000 Kazakhs, shortly after the revolution, sought asylum in Sinkiang. However, the migration of the Kazakhs soon came to a halt when the Russian Communists, under Lenin's leadership, altered their tactics and sought to pose as champions of the smaller ethnic groups, including the other Turkic peoples of Central Asia.

This change of tactic would also be used to further Soviet penetration of Sinkiang. When, by the middle of the 1920's, Soviet authority had been established throughout the Aral Sea Basin, Russian interest in Sinkiang revived. An agreement with the local Chinese governor in 1924 permitted the Soviets to establish consulates at Altai (Sharashune), Chuguchak, Kuldja, Kashgar, and Urumchi. Theaters and libraries were also opened, becoming quickly centers of Communist propaganda. By the end of the decade, the whole of Sinkiang's foreign trade was in Soviet hands. The completion in 1930 of the Turkestan-Siberian Railway, south from Semipalatinsk to Alma-Ata, assisted materially the Soviet economic offensive in Sinkiang.

The relative calm that had prevailed throughout Sinkiang, in the 1920's, came to an end in 1931. That year, when Japan invaded Manchuria, was equally critical for Sinkiang. Not only did a mass migration of thousands of Chinese into the province from the east occur, but the native Dungans revolted against the local Chinese administration. Though ethnically Chinese, the Dungans nevertheless had a different way of life, based in part on their belief in Islam. The Chinese governor was unable to bring the revolt under control and was compelled to accept Soviet assistance. In return, he granted extensive privileges to the Soviets, which included major commercial concessions and the right of free movement throughout the province. Sovsintorg, the Soviet-Sinkiang Trading Agency, immediately established agencies in eight key centers in Sinkiang.

Shortly thereafter, another armed uprising occurred in the oases of the Tarim Basin, this time led by Turkic-speaking Muslims, who, tacitly supported by the British, proclaimed at Kashgar a Muslim Republic of East Turkestan. Turkic forces laid siege to Urumchi. The new Chinese governor, General Sheng Shih-ts'ai, was compelled to seek Russian assistance, which led ultimately to the defeat of the rebels in July, 1934. Such was the ethnocentrism of the native peoples of Sinkiang, that, in spite of their common Islamic faith, they were unable to make common cause against the much-disliked Chinese overlords.

In the meantime, the political situation in Sinkiang was further complicated by events in adjacent Kazakhstan. When Stalin began his drive for all-out collectivization, at least 250,000 Kazakhs moved south and east, with their herds and flocks. Some went on over the mountains into India. Others attempted to settle in Chinese territory. Yet, in spite of the activities of the Russian Communists, the Kazakhs probably still regarded the Chinese as traditional enemies. Their arrival in Sinkiang was not, therefore, a stabilizing event.

In order to secure Soviet military assistance in putting down the Turkic revolt, Chinese Governor Sheng, who was both a professed Communist and politically oriented toward the Soviet Union, agreed to major concessions. Without obtaining the consent of the Chinese Nationalist government in Nanking, he surrendered to the Soviets a monopoly of the province's exports of raw materials. Hence, from 1932 to 1943, when the Russians were compelled to withdraw, Sinkiang was little more than a Soviet satellite. Red Army garrisons were much in evidence throughout the province.

During that period, the Russians built up a large network of Communist institutions, headed by Soviet advisers, who crossed the border in the guise of specialists or even anti-Bolshevik *emigrés*. At the same time, the Soviets made strong efforts to awaken the national consciousness of the peoples of Sinkiang, in order to use them against the Chinese Nationalists. In this connection, to propagandize the natives, well-indoctrinated Turkestanis were sent in from Soviet Central Asia. The Chinese Kazakhs, it is reported, like the other peoples, for the most part took the overtures of friendship by the Russians at their face value, in spite of what they might have learned from the Russian Kazakhs. Thus, the events from 1931 to 1934 tended to stimulate on the one hand Pan-Turkist feeling, and on the other, Uighur and Kazakh nationalism, weakening further earlier Pan-Islamist ties.

Domination of Sinkiang's commerce had been a major objective of Soviet policy. Of even greater importance to the Soviets was complete control over the exploitation of Sinkiang's mineral wealth. In 1934, Soviet geologists began surveying the province, and maps of its resources were prepared. The Soviets were particularly interested in finding oil, while Sinkiang's output of tungsten enabled the Soviets to cut back on imports from other parts of China.

Governor Sheng's policies and increasing Soviet penetration of all aspects of life in Sinkiang led to a revolt in 1936. But the uprising failed. Thousands were massacred, and others fled into Kansu, pursued by the Red Army. In 1937, another popular revolt broke out in Yarkend, aimed at driving both the Russians and Chinese out. Russian troops helped put down the revolt, but again the bloodshed was considerable. These revolts in no way weakened Soviet influence in, or control of, Sinkiang. If anything, the military occupation grew. In 1940, an agreement between Governor Sheng and the Soviets gave the latter additional privileges in the province, including the right to explore for zinc and other minerals, and to construct a communications network.

Yet, in 1940, still another revolt broke out in Sinkiang, this time in Altai province among the Kazakhs. The northwest possesses the richest mineral deposits in Sinkiang. The region was of special interest to the Russians. Yet, despite the efforts of both the Russians and Governor Sheng, the revolt continued for several years.

Meanwhile, the outbreak of World War II was about to have a very important influence on events in Sinkiang. In June, 1941, the Nazis invaded the USSR, while in the following December, the Japanese attacked Pearl Harbor, bringing the USA into the conflict.

Governor Sheng suddenly turned against his Soviet "advisers," and sought an understanding with Chiang Kai-shek, at this time allied with and supported by the USA in the common fight against Japan. Sheng's abrupt about-face, along with the disorders in the Altai region, weakened the Soviet position in Sinkiang. Finally, in 1943, as a result of German pressure in the west, the Soviets were forced to withdraw their forces from Sinkiang. Kuomintang troops were dispatched to put down the native uprisings and Governor Sheng was replaced. The year 1943, therefore, marks the beginning of Chinese Nationalist rule in Sinkiang in a real sense, but it was too brief and difficult a time for effective control to be imposed.

There was no reason why the native peoples of Sinkiang should welcome the Kuomintang. Prior to his removal, Governor Sheng had begun to implement a policy toward the nationalities, which he hoped would find favor with Chiang Kai-shek. This policy reflected the "Greater Chinese Theory," subscribed to by Chiang, according to which the nationalities of China were all one nation and one race, that is to say, Chinese. Thus, whereas, before, Sheng had permitted Soviet encouragement of local feeling, he now began to suppress local nationalisms. With the resident Communists, he was even more ruthless. Indeed, he is reported to have eliminated all Chinese Communists in Sinkiang in 1942, including Mao Tse-tung's brother. But Sheng's sudden embrace of the Nationalist cause could not keep him in office. His successor, on the other hand, announced that he had come to bring local autonomy to all, but few were convinced, and the native uprisings continued.

From the end of 1944 on, the situation in Sinkiang was one of considerable confusion. The anti-Chinese revolt which flared up at Kuldja (Ining) in November was aided by the Soviets. Well-armed and equipped, the rebel forces drove the Chinese Nationalist troops out of northwestern Sinkiang, winning a major victory at Wusu in the summer of 1945. Immediately, a Revolutionary Republic of Eastern Turkestan was proclaimed. The Soviets offered to mediate the dispute, and the rebels, on the verge of capturing Urumchi, surprisingly acquiesced. Obviously, the Russians were calling the tune, too.

The efforts to establish effective Kuomintang administration in China while carrying on a struggle with the Chinese Communists elsewhere would not permit Chiang Kai-shek to deploy sufficient resources to remote Sinkiang. Time had run out. It would be, as we shall see, only a matter of weeks after major Communist victories in the east that Sinkiang would fall into Chinese Communist hands in the west.

III

The Zone of Stabilization

THE PERIOD OF 1945-49

I<small>T WAS</small> generally believed in the United States, after Germany's defeat in World War II seemed apparent, that the war with Japan in the Far East would go on for many months after the cessation of European hostilities. The prolongation of the war, too, it was believed, would cost the lives of many Americans, particularly if and when the invasion of the Japanese home islands occurred. Hence, U.S. military strategists were eager to have Soviet participation with a view to bringing the Pacific war to an early close. The Soviet Union, throughout the entire conflict, had remained neutral in the Pacific, devoting her resources primarily to the European theatre. Thus, in 1944, much effort was made to discover how and on what terms the USSR could be brought into the war against Japan.

As part of its vision of the post-war world, the United States looked forward to the emergence of a strong China, united under Nationalist control, and recognized by the USSR and Great Britain as an equal in international deliberations. Above all, the United States looked forward to a China friendly to the West and particularly to the United States itself. Yet, in planning the military campaign in the Pacific, the Western Allies did not carefully anticipate the political implications of Japan's unconditional surrender. At any rate, it was assumed, by some American leaders primarily, that the powers, in an effort to create a free, new world, would not be swayed by matters of selfish, national interest. Certainly, during the war, no carefully conceived plans had been made with respect to the future of the Chinese borderlands. Generally it was agreed that Chinese sovereignty should be established over those territories which had been taken by Japan. But what of the traditional ambitions of others in the Far East; above all, what of China's giant neighbor, the Soviet Union? The Soviet Union would be keenly interested in the details of any settlement with Japan. Further, Russia's entry into the Pacific war against Japan would require an understanding of specific post-war objectives, largely as the price of her entry.

The Declaration of November, 1943, which brought together Roosevelt, Churchill and Chiang Kai-shek in Cairo, had promised the return to China of all territories taken by Japan—that is, Manchuria, Formosa, and the Pescadores Islands. Although Stalin unofficially approved the declaration, the Western Allies were dismayed, in the months that followed, to learn of the extent of Soviet ambitions which were presented as the price for Soviet participation in the war. Clearly the cost to China would be considerable, but the Soviets, like their Allied counterparts, undoubtedly reckoned on a prolonged conflict with Japan.

Without consulting Chiang Kai-shek aforehand, the United States, Great Britain, and the Soviet Union agreed secretly at Yalta, in February, 1945, on the means and conditions whereby the latter would enter the war. The terms of the agreement dealt particularly with the Manchurian and Mongolian borderlands. The Yalta Agreement, as far as the Soviet Union was concerned, in effect reversed the decision of 1905. The Soviets were granted a lease on Port Arthur as a naval base and recognition of their pre-eminent position in the commercial port of Dairen, which was to be internationalized. The Chinese Changchun Railway, that is, the combined Chinese Eastern and South Manchurian Railways, was to be operated by a joint Soviet-Chinese Company. Further, Southern Sakhalin was to be restored to the Soviet Union and, *in addition,* the Soviets were to be accorded the Japanese Kurile Islands, which had never been Russian before, to protect Soviet outlets to the Pacific. As for Outer Mongolia, or the Mongolian People's Republic, the status quo was to be preserved. The legality of the Yalta Agreement with respect to

Chinese territory would depend, however, on a Sino-Soviet treaty, which the Western Allies would help to bring about.

In spite of U.S. concern that the war against Japan would not be readily won, the rapidity and completeness of the Japanese collapse came as a surprise. No one in informed circles in the U.S. could foresee the ultimate impact of the atomic bomb. Hiroshima was attacked on August 6, 1945, the Soviets entered the war on August 8, quickly sweeping into Manchuria and, on August 14, the Japanese emperor called for peace. Undoubtedly, the speed with which the war was brought to a successful conclusion surprised the Red Army as well as the Western forces.

It was under these circumstances that, on the same day Japan surrendered, the Sino-Soviet Treaty was signed. Under the terms of the treaty, the USSR pledged to recognize and to support the Nationalist government and to respect China's sovereignty over Manchuria and Sinkiang. Port Arthur would be used as a joint naval base while Dairen would function as a free port under Chinese civil administration. It should be emphasized that the treaty, by implication, was aimed at Japan, the common enemy in the Far East in the near future. In return for Soviet promises, Chiang Kai-shek pledged recognition of the independence of the Mongolian People's Republic if the Mongols themselves expressed such a desire in a plebiscite, which would be held at a later date.

In spite of the confusion at the time, it seems likely that the Soviet leaders assumed that the Nationalists would rule post-war China. There is no evidence to suggest that the Soviets anticipated that a Communist revolution would succeed within the foreseeable future. Hence, it is difficult to get a clear impression of what the Soviets had intended to do in Manchuria and Sinkiang. At any rate, the coming to power of the Chinese Communists in 1949 radically altered the entire Far Eastern situation and brought a superior organization to the important Chinese borderlands.

In 1927 Chiang Kai-shek, who in the early years of his government had had the support of the Chinese Communist Party, turned on the Communists and drove them into the hills of south-central

China. Their numbers depleted, their hope of capturing the urban masses gone, the Chinese Communists were compelled to work out their own tactics in the countryside. These, as we now know, came to be based on the peasants and not on the proletariat in the strict Marxist tradition. Steadily mounting Nationalist pressure by 1935, however, forced the Communists to undertake their historic "Long March" into northern Shensi where they established a new base. There, Mao Tse-tung rose to undisputed leadership of the party.

It was the Japanese invasion of China that ultimately made possible the emergence of the Communists as a major factor in Chinese politics. The war led to the formation of a United Front, an uneasy truce which, from 1937 on, enabled Mao to implement his policy of "70 per cent self-development, 20 per cent compromise, and 10 per cent fighting the Japanese." Meanwhile as the struggle with Japan continued on into World War II, it brought increasing devastation to China and the war-weary Chinese people. When the conflict ended in 1945, the country was prostrate, but the people were optimistic of the future. The situation, however, offered promising opportunities to the Communists, particularly when the Nationalists seemed unable to cope with the intricate problems of restoring order to the occupied and war-ravaged areas of the country. Attempts on the part of the United States to bring some kind of unity to China through the formation of a coalition government failed. The civil war that had been latent since 1927 and had occasionally erupted in hostilities broke out afresh and swept over the northern provinces of the country.

Toward the end of World War II no one could envisage what the "brave, new world" would be like once hostilities had ended, but there were hopeful expectations that man, as a result of the wanton slaughter and destruction that had overtaken the world twice within the twentieth century, would plan a settlement that could handle, effectively and amicably, disputes among nations as they arose. There were those, too, who, from their study of history, were not inclined to look for any radical departure in the conduct of world affairs. Such a person was George Kennan, long a careful student and analyst of the Soviet Union, and in 1945 U.S. chargé d'affaires in Moscow. In a telegram to Averill Harriman in Washington on April 23, 1945, he indicated what he anticipated post-war Soviet policy in Asia to be.[1] "I am persuaded," he said, "that in the future Soviet policy respecting China will continue what it has been in the recent past: a fluid resilient policy directed at the achievement of maximum power with minimum responsibility . . . the exertion of pressure in various areas in direct proportion to their strategic importance and their proximity to the Soviet frontier . . . domination of the provinces of China in Central Asia contiguous to the Soviet frontier."

The Soviet intervention in the Chinese borderlands during the period 1945-49 clearly demonstrated the insight that Kennan revealed in his telegram.

MANCHURIA

The Red Army encountered little opposition from the Japanese in its sweep over Manchuria in mid-August, 1945. After a minimum of fighting, the Japanese forces surrendered. Red Army troops took over the railways, the industries, and the ports; widespread looting occurred and whatever could be transported back to the Soviet Union was confiscated. In this way, the Soviets stripped systematically the Manchurian industrial base of all its essentials. The cost of restoring the industry, which, because it was located in the south, had not been damaged during the Japanese war (although further wrecked during the Civil War), was subsequently estimated at $2,000 million U.S. dollars. This ruthless destruction of the Manchurian "Ruhr," as western historians have since pointed out, raises the question of whether the Soviets expected an early victory of the Chinese Communists. At any rate, the Red Army violated the Yalta Agreement by remaining in Manchuria after the hostilities with Japan had ended. When they did withdraw in April 1946, they did so only after completing their rape of the productive province and not until Manchuria had been thoroughly infiltrated by Chinese Communist units armed largely with confiscated Japanese weapons. The Nationalist armies moved into the cities of Manchuria, but the Commu-

[1] Allen S. Whiting and General Sheng Shih-ts'ai, *Sinkiang: Pawn or Pivot?* East Lansing: Michigan State University Press, 1958, p. 108.

nists spread throughout the countryside. Unquestionably, the presence of Soviet troops facilitated the spread of Communist power in Manchuria, especially in the north and center. In its dealings with the Nationalists, the Soviet government attempted, for the most part, to be correct: yet it did nothing to assist the Nationalists in establishing an administration in a Manchuria that the Red Army had crippled. What is not so clear throughout these months, however, is the nature of the relations between the Soviet and Chinese Communist Parties.

Throughout 1946, nevertheless, Chiang was able to control the situation. But largely because of the Nationalists' inability to establish and maintain effective control of Manchuria, the balance began tipping in 1947-48 in favor of the Communists. By the end of 1948, the Communists had occupied Mukden, the last Nationalist stronghold in southern Manchuria, and the civil war then moved south of the Great Wall. Early in 1949 Peking fell and, by the summer, Shanghai. On October 1, the establishment of a new Communist government was announced, which was promptly recognized the next day by the USSR. By the end of the year, all mainland China had come under Communist rule, and the Nationalists were established on their island stronghold, Taiwan (Formosa). Early in 1950, after a visit by Mao to Moscow, China and Russia abrogated their old treaties and entered into new agreements.

MONGOLIA

At Yalta, in early 1945, it will be recalled, Stalin had secured an agreement from the United States and Great Britain that the MPR would become independent of China in law as well as in fact. The Sino-Soviet Treaty later that year pledged China to recognize the independence of Mongolia in her existing borders, to be confirmed later by a plebiscite in that republic. The plebiscite was held on October 20, 1945, supervised by the Soviets, and the Mongolians voted almost 100 per cent for independence. In January, 1946, Nationalist China recognized the independence of the MPR. Thus, a quarter of a century after its "war of liberation," the MPR was legally separated from China, under whose tutelage it had been since the end of the 17th century. But this independence, in effect, had little meaning for the Mongols themselves, who had fallen under Soviet domination.

In 1947, Mongolia adopted a Five Year Plan of the Soviet type and in 1949 amended its 1940 constitution more closely along Soviet lines. Russian cultural influence also increased, particularly when the Cyrillic or Russian alphabet was officially introduced to replace the traditional Mongol script. Finally, in 1949, the Soviets undertook to construct a railway south from the Trans-Siberian to Ulan Bator. In the immediate post-war years, therefore, Soviet control of the life of the republic intensified. It was primarily because of a recognition of this situation that the application of the MPR for admission to the United Nations in 1946, and again in 1947, was vetoed by the United States and Nationalist China.

SINKIANG

Under the terms of the Sino-Soviet Treaty of August, 1945, the USSR promised to respect China's sovereignty in Sinkiang. Stalin asserted he had no territorial claims on China. Yet clearly the Soviet Union was interested in Sinkiang—and particularly in the Eastern Turkestan Republic which held that portion of the province containing the richest mineral resources.

In the agreement that was finally signed with the native rebel forces in Urumchi in June, 1946, major concessions to regional autonomy were granted by Chiang. In effect, this meant a tacit recognition of a Soviet sphere in Sinkiang. The concessions, as Allen Whiting pointed out in his book, *Sinkiang: Pawn or Pivot?*, represented a search "for a compromise solution which might restrain Soviet backing of the rival Chinese Communists" elsewhere in China.[2] But in the months that followed, conflicts developed within the rebel republic, and ultimately the name of the republic was dropped.

In the meantime Uighur nationalists in the Tarim Basin took advantage of Chinese preoccupation with the Kuldja rebellion to demand an independent Turkestani state. The leaders of the move-

[2] *Ibid.*, p. 110.

ment envisaged an authoritarian state, embracing not only the Turks of Sinkiang, but also their cousins in Soviet Central Asia, including in their dream even the Yakuts of northeastern Siberia. Though anti-Communist as well as anti-Russian in outlook, the Pan-Turkists established friendly relations with the rebels in Kuldja. The Kuomintang was unable to deal with this new threat; above all, Chiang did not oppose the movement, probably because he feared that he might push the Uighurs into close association with leftist elements. At any rate, the Chinese Nationalists came to terms with the Uighurs and, in May, 1947, appointed a Uighur to head the regional government. However, this act did not provide a solution, for the governor was more Uighur than Kuomintang. Indeed, the governor went so far as to seek outside support for his ideas by establishing relations with the United States mission in Urumchi. Finally, in December, 1948, Chiang removed the governor, but the internal political situation in China proper had so changed that little if any action could be taken in Sinkiang.

There were additional troubles for the Kuomintang in Sinkiang. In September, 1946, Soviet and Mongol troops invaded the Altai district of Sinkiang, creating the so-called Pietashan Affair. The invading forces justified their attack, claiming the area was rightfully a part of Outer Mongolia, and had been so as late as 1919. Because the Mongols of the Altai had not fought alongside the Outer Mongols in 1911 to oust the Chinese from the plateau, the new Chinese republican government had detached the Altai district from Mongolia and added it to Sinkiang. The Russians denied their participation in the affair, but the Chinese Nationalists denounced Soviet strategy and denied outer Mongolian claims.

While the Nationalists refused to enter into any new agreements with the Soviets for joint economic development of Sinkiang, they nevertheless, in May, 1949, surrendered virtual control over the air route between Alma Ata and Hami, via Urumchi. Such was Soviet policy that, while the Chinese Communists were rapidly advancing throughout China proper, the Russians still found it wise to seek or force concessions from the Nationalists in Sinkiang.

Finally, on September 26, 1949, as Chinese Communist units were approaching from the east, the Chinese governor of Sinkiang declared the province a part of Communist China. On October 13, the troops entered Sinkiang. The armed local rebel forces were disbanded, and their leaders purged. Others despaired of their position. When the Communists took Urumchi, some 3000 Kazakhs began to move out. Fleeing southward, they passed through the Tien Shan and skirted Lob Nor, before heading into the rugged Altyn Tagh. But of the 3000 herdsmen who left Sinkiang, only a small remnant reached India late in 1951 after a horrifying experience.

1950 TO THE PRESENT

The establishment of a Chinese Communist regime in Peking marked the beginning of a new era in Asia, and one which would have far-reaching implications for the entire world. It would mean, above all, the emergence of a new set of political geographical relationships, based to an important degree on the ideological unity between the two Communist powers, the Soviet Union and the People's Republic of China. These new relationships were to have, in the decade following 1950, a significant bearing on the development of the Chinese territories bordering the USSR.

Hitherto Russian expansion in East and Inner Asia, whether of the tsarist or Soviet variety, had occurred mainly at the expense of a weak and disorganized China. Indeed, the very weakness of China had encouraged and facilitated Russian expansion, no less than it had stimulated the imperial rivalry there of Japan, Germany, France and Great Britain. The Communist success, however, brought to an end foreign overseas intervention in Chinese affairs. Equally significant, it compelled the Soviets to reassess their policy toward the Chinese state. Thereafter, Soviet strategy in Asia would have to contend with the fact of effective Chinese control in the borderlands. But this control would now be imposed by the Communist Party of China, ideologically linked to the Communist Party of the Soviet Union. Hence, Chinese Communist ascendancy has meant the end of the role traditionally played by Manchuria and Sinkiang as pawns in Asia. It has resulted also in the emergence of a recognized Chinese interest in Outer Mongolia where for nearly thirty years the Soviet Union was paramount.

Immediately following the revolution, the new Chinese regime took a number of steps to organize and to integrate both Sinkiang and Manchuria. Soviet influence and control which had survived or re-emerged there after World War II were, by a series of agreements, gradually reduced and finally liquidated. Although Soviet and Chinese Communist maps and atlases reveal boundary discrepancies in the Pamirs and at the confluence of the Amur and Ussuri Rivers, these do not appear to be serious issues, nor of enough importance to disturb the ideological unity of the two powers or the stability of either the Inner Asian or the Far Eastern borderlands. News dispatches out of Formosa and India from time to time have mentioned opposition of the native Turks to the Chinese in Sinkiang, but other reports suggest convincingly that the Communists are capable of handling any disorder that might develop there. Hence, for the first time in decades—and indeed one might argue, in history—Sinkiang and Manchuria have become truly oriented toward China.

In the Mongolian People's Republic, on the other hand, the Soviets have been able since 1950 to preserve their hegemony. Yet, the Chinese Communists were quick to follow their recognition of Mongolian "independence" with the establishment of an impressive and sizable embassy in Ulan Bator. Cultural exchange and economic aid agreements have resulted in a large influx of Chinese workers to assist in major construction projects. Chinese interest in Mongolia is a fact, and the Soviets have recognized this and apparently are willing to accept joint economic development of the MPR. What they might do if their pre-eminent role in Mongolia were challenged, or if the political status of Mongolia were questioned by the Chinese, is a matter only for speculation. Within Mongolia, the presence of large numbers of Chinese (workers and their families) does not seem to disturb the Mongols, in spite of traditional antipathy, but it is impossible, of course, to determine the true feelings of the Mongols. At any rate, the Mongols are in a position to benefit from both the USSR and the CPR, so long as unity and friendship prevail. Undoubtedly, it is this unity which has minimized the importance of the Mongolian-Chinese boundary discrepancies. The skirmishes that occurred, for example, between the Chinese Nationalists and the Mongols in the Altai region ended when the Communists took over Sinkiang.

In recognizing officially the independence of the MPR, the Chinese Communists also gave tacit approval to the Soviet annexation of the Mongol province known as Tannu-Tuva. At the time of formal incorporation of the territory into the USSR in 1944, Tannu-Tuva possessed some strategic value for the Russians. Under Russian control, it afforded a shorter and generally more favorable border with the MPR or with Nationalist China, should the latter succeed in gaining full possession of Outer Mongolia. Moreover, the upland region, bounded on the north by the Sayan Mountains and on the south by the Tannu-Ola Range, lies astride the most direct route between western Siberia and the western Mongolian centers of Kobdo and Uliassutai. But perhaps of even more value to the Russians is the mineral wealth of the region. Not only is Tannu-Tuva, or the Tuva ASSR, rich in coal, but it also has important deposits of asbestos, salt, gold, and copper.

Development of these resources, however, continues to remain in the first stages. While a good motor road connects the capital, Kyzyl, with Abakan to the north of the Sayan, the region still has, as far as is known, no direct rail link with the rest of the Soviet Union.

Of the 172,000 inhabitants of the oblast, at least 80,000 are Russians, the bulk of whom live in the capital and other large centers. It would seem, therefore, that Tuva has become irrevocably Russian.

It should be realized that the Chinese Communists are dedicated to world revolution and internationalism, and these objectives they share with their Soviet counterparts. All other interests have, for the most part, since 1950, played a subordinate role. In order to promote world communism (and Sino-Soviet interests), the leaders of both countries have pledged themselves to friendship. The advantages that ensue will continue to outweigh considerations of a purely national character. The adherence of the Chinese mainland to the Communist bloc presently led by the USSR has enhanced the strength of the bloc, if measured only in legions; at the same time, the alliance has made possible Soviet aid to China in its vast program of reconstruction.

THE WITHDRAWAL OF THE SOVIETS FROM MANCHURIA AND SINKIANG

Shortly after the formation of the new government in Peking in September-October, 1949, Mao Tse-tung left for Moscow on his first visit to the USSR. His negotiations there with Premier Stalin, culminating in February, 1950, in a Treaty of Friendship, Alliance and Mutual Aid, laid the basis for a new Sino-Soviet state relationship. The agreements held a special significance for Manchuria and Sinkiang.

Although the Soviets did not agree to an immediate departure from Manchuria, they did make concessions. Until a peace treaty had been signed with Japan, but not later than the end of 1952, the Soviets would remain on in Manchuria. They would share administration with the Chinese of the Changchun Railway. They would garrison Port Arthur, but the base would be used jointly with the Chinese. Dairen, the main port of the southern terminus of the Manchurian railway system, would rest solely in the hands of a Chinese civil administration. Several joint-stock enterprises were also agreed on, including a shipbuilding and repair company at Dairen.

With respect to Sinkiang, the Soviets and the Chinese agreed in March, 1950, on the establishment of similar joint-stock companies to exploit oil and nonferrous metals. The capital, control and the profits were to be shared for 30 years. Some western observers have claimed that these joint-stock enterprises represented a continuation of Soviet interest in Sinkiang's resources. Undoubtedly this is true; yet, at the same time, in the early years of the Chinese Communist takeover in Sinkiang, the Chinese needed whatever assistance the Soviets could or would give, especially since the latter in past decades had already begun operations there. At any rate, it is clear that the Chinese intended to make Sinkiang Chinese, for in March, 1950,

Peking announced a program for large-scale immigration into the western province.

Finally, the agreements reached in Moscow in March, 1950, pertained also to the organization and operation of civilian airlines between Peking and Chita, Peking and Irkutsk, and Peking and Alma Ata.

In 1952, since no peace treaty with Japan had been signed, the Soviets complied with the terms of the 1950 treaty and transferred, without compensation, the Changchun Railway to sole Chinese administration. Soviet forces, however, remained in Port Arthur, largely because of the Korean War and, reportedly, at China's suggestion and request. Two years later, following the visit of Khrushchev and Bulganin to Peking, the Soviets agreed to transfer their shares in the Manchurian joint-stock companies to China, and in 1955 they withdrew their garrison from Port Arthur. Thus, ten years after they entered Manchuria to fight the Japanese and five years after the Chinese Communist victory over the Nationalists there, Soviet forces were withdrawn to Russian territory. Apart from the fact that Soviet engineers and other technical personnel remained to assist in the reconstruction of Manchuria, the Soviets have acknowledged Chinese supremacy in Manchuria.

During the Khrushchev mission to China, it was agreed that the Soviets would transfer to China their shares in the Sinkiang joint mining companies. These companies had not accomplished very much beyond planning activities and training Chinese and native Sinkiang personnel. The greatest progress was made in the oil industry, including considerable drilling and the construction of an automatic cracking plant equipped with Soviet machinery. The transfer of shares began in 1955, and the companies were reorganized as Chinese state-owned enterprises. Finally, as a result of an agreement in October, 1954, the Soviets and Chinese began construction of a new rail line, which would link the Turk-Sib Railway with the Lanchow-Sinkiang Railway that the Chinese had begun building in 1952. Thus, as in Manchuria, the Soviets by 1955 had surrendered their "sphere of influence" and had allowed the Chinese to take over full control and direction of Sinkiang's economic development.

CHINESE COMMUNIST REORGANIZATION OF THE BORDERLANDS

Political Reorganization. Like the USSR, the CPR is a land of different national or ethnic groups. The diversity in China, however, is considerably less than in the Soviet Union. The Han-Chinese, like their Slavic or Russian counterparts to the north, predominate. But whereas the Slavs constitute three-fourths of the USSR's population, and the Russians alone slightly less, the Han-Chinese account for 94 per cent of China's population.

The national minorities of China inhabit primarily the border areas, that is, around the periphery of China Proper. The border territories, especially on the north and east, as we have seen, are large and strategic and, in the drier areas, sparsely settled. Rich in resources, too, these territories have remained, with the exception of Manchuria, undeveloped. Yet, whatever material progress there has been, has been prompted, certainly until recently, by Russians or Japanese, but not by the native peoples themselves or by the Chinese. It should be kept in mind, too, that the national groups of the borderlands are related to similar ethnic and culture groups in the Soviet Union. Moreover, to add another complicating factor, some of these peoples, notably the Muslim Uighurs of Sinkiang, have traditionally been anti-Chinese, and even the semi-nomadic Inner Mongols have had cause to resent the encroachment of the Chinese farmer on their ancient grazing lands.

As they were consolidating their hold on the mainland, the Chinese Communists were compelled to make concessions to the minority groups in an attempt to allay their fears and suspicions. When, however, they had secured effective control, they introduced a policy, based on that evolved in the Soviet Union, designed to eliminate national aspirations and in effect to destroy the bases of the native cultures.

The nationalities policy involves the setting up of a hierarchy of national territorial units to represent fixed and stable ethnic groups in an attempt to create the illusion of local or regional autonomy. Within such territories, native culture forms are permitted to survive even though the social fabric is remodeled along lines determined by the party leaders. The net result of such a policy, if carried to the ultimate, means the death of any true national identity and of the traditions of a proud people inherited from time immemorial. Whatever promotes "friendship" and "unity" between the minorities and the predominant group is permitted and encouraged; whatever reveals basic historic antagonisms between the peoples and stimulates the desire for separation and national independence is suppressed and destroyed, often brutally. Moreover, the party leaders are not above rewriting history to "verify" their point of view should it be necessary.

Constitutionally, the Soviet Union is a union of the federal type, consisting at present of 15 republics. These have been established for compact national groups that total a million or more and who live along the borders of the country. The fact of their location is important, according to the Soviet constitution, because it permits the people to secede. This right, however, is purely a theoretical one; to date, no republics have seceded nor is the desire for secession ever allowed to express itself. Prior to their victory in 1949, the Chinese Communists may have entertained the idea of a federal structure for China, but the republic is today a unitary state. Because of the overwhelming size of the Han-Chinese majority, the Chinese Communists may conceivably have felt that the minority groups were not important enough numerically to warrant supporting the myth of a federation of free and equal peoples. At any rate, within the unitary state framework, the Chinese have established a hierarchy of national regions, but it is considerably less elaborate than that in existence in the Soviet Union.

At the highest level of the structure are the autonomous regions, or ch'u, which may be compared to the Union republics, except for the fact that the regions do not have the right to secede. Next in the hierarchy are the autonomous districts, or chow, and below the chow, the autonomous areas, or hsien, and banners, or ch'i. The present political-administrative delineation of China has come about mainly since 1953.

In Manchuria, from August, 1949, to November, 1952, there existed what in effect amounted to an autonomous Communist regime. The

Northeast People's Government had been established, because Manchuria was the most advanced, from the point of view of Communist power consolidation. The territory was then divided into five provinces and a national region. Subsequently, in November, 1952, after the Northeast Government had been abolished, Manchuria was reorganized. In June, 1954, a second reorganization followed, but Manchuria was not accorded national autonomy. Obviously, the complete Sinification of the Manchu peoples there (today numbering about two million) as a result of the considerable Chinese migration was an important element working against autonomy. But the overriding industrial importance to China of Manchuria, as well as other political considerations, was more telling. Consequently, the Chinese Communists rejected the term "Manchuria," and now refer to the region as Tungpei, or the Northeast.

The drier western part, the Khingan region, was detached from old Manchuria, and, with its Mongol population, given to an enlarged Inner Mongolia. The Northeast, therefore, includes three provinces: Heilungkiang, Kirin, and Liaoning. Heilungkiang, the largest province, faces the Soviet Far East across the Amur and Ussuri Rivers. The province of Kirin to the south borders in part on the Korean People's Republic. South of Kirin is Liaoning, which includes the industrial core of old Manchuria. Nevertheless, the Northeast encompasses some 300,000 sq. miles, and contains over 40 million inhabitants, mainly Chinese. Several autonomous areas have been established for the scattered groups of Mongols that remain, while some half million culturally-tenacious Koreans, along the eastern border of Kirin, form the Yen-Pien Autonomous District.

As early as 1947, the Communists proclaimed an Inner Mongolian Autonomous Region, but in the decade that followed, its boundaries were considerably modified, as the region was expanded in size. Of all the minority groups, the Inner Mongols have undoubtedly been courted the most—and for a variety of interesting political reasons. When the Japanese occupied parts of Inner Mongolia, they made a conscious effort to win the favor of the Mongols—and not without some success. In the immediate postwar period, the proclamation of the Inner Mongolian Autonomous Region undoubtedly helped win the Mongols to the side of the Communists. Yet the Chinese in Inner Mongolia outnumber the Mongols by at least five to one, while in the southeast, where most of the Chinese agriculturalists have settled, the ratio is probably even greater. Nevertheless, there are more Mongols in the CPR than in the MPR or in the USSR, and they are identified through the autonomous region. The construction in 1953 of a tomb for Genghis Khan in Inner Mongolia also seems to be a part of the overall appeal to the Mongols, for among all Mongols, the story of the great warrior-leader remains very much alive.

To the west of Inner Mongolia, beyond Kansu, is ethnically-complex Sinkiang. When control had finally been effected there, perhaps sometime in 1955, the Sinkiang-Uighur Autonomous Region was created in recognition of the predominant national group, the Uighurs.

However, like the Russian Communists, the Chinese Communists have rejected the Pan-Turic argument that all the Turkic-speaking peoples of both Soviet Central Asia and Sinkiang belong to one single nation. Rather, the position adopted in both the USSR and the CPR is that the Turkic peoples constitute several groups. The Communists stress the historic differences between the various groups involved, the Kazakhs, the Uzbeks, the Kirgiz, the Uighurs, and others, ignoring the similarities that exist, or the feelings of mutual kinship that may exist. Thus, within the Sinkiang-Uighur Autonomous Region have been set up subordinate units representing non-Uighur minorities. There are, in addition, other subordinate units for the Mongols, as well as for the Tadzhiks, the Sibos, and the Huis Dungans). Until recent years, the number of Chinese settlers in Sinkiang has remained relatively small. But the Chinese Communists have encouraged migration, and it may be expected that before long the Chinese will outnumber the natives. The exploitation of the rich mineral base, land reclamation, improved communications, and industrial development should all work to the disadvantage of the region's traditional cultures.

In 1956, as part of its program of indoctrination, the Peking regime announced that it would adopt the Cyrillic (Russian) alphabet for the Mongolian and Turkic languages of Inner Mongolia and Sinkiang. This would have made it possible for the Uighurs and the Inner Mongols to read materials published in the Soviet Union for the respective ethnic groups there. Perhaps it was believed in Peking that this would, in effect, speed up indoctrination of China's minorities, and conversely enable the Chinese to influence thinking among the Soviet minorities. At any rate, the plan was dropped not long after, when Premier Chou En-lai announced that the Latin script rather than the Cyrillic would be introduced for all of China's languages. This change was confirmed two years later, in 1960, when it was reported [3] that the Sinkiang-Uighur Regional People's Council had given its approval to replacing with Latin the Arabic script traditionally employed in Uighur and Kazakh writing. The change-over was expected to take from three to five years. Without doubt, the Latinization of the languages of China would facilitate communication within the republic, but it would create a barrier for the peoples on either side of the Sino-Mongolian-Soviet boundary. Ease of communication via the Cyrillic alphabet throughout the Sino-Soviet borderlands could lead to indoctrination, but it could just as easily lead to the Russification of China's minorities. Yet, the Mongols, Uighurs and other minority groups have been told that if they wish advancement within the new China, that is possible only through the study of Chinese. To encourage this, the Chinese have opened new schools throughout the border territories, where Chinese is taught. It has been made sufficiently clear to all that Chinese is to be the official language everywhere.

Economic Reorganization and Development. During their occupation of Manchuria (Manchukuo), the Japanese erected an industrial base well in advance of the rest of China. Not only does the region possess large reserves of coal, oil shale, iron ore and other minerals, but its upland forests are valuable, the energy potential of its rivers is considerable, and its agriculture capable of producing surpluses. The Japanese greatly increased the output of fuels and minerals,

[3] *The New York Times,* March 27, 1960.

built power stations, double-tracked and extended the railways, and erected a complex of manufacturing establishments second in the Far East only to the home industry of Japan itself.

The economic importance of Manchuria to China was fully appreciated by both the Chinese Nationalists and Communists in 1945. Chiang Kai-shek was determined to establish Nationalist control there, but was frustrated by the Soviets, and finally lost the cream of his army in the struggle with the Communists. The latter won Manchuria but were compelled to accept, without complaint, an industrial machine that had been crippled by the Red Army. Furthermore, as the Japanese workers returned to their homes in Japan, the Chinese were left without the skills to operate the establishments. Thus, the new Communist rulers of Manchuria were confronted with an enormous task, that of rebuilding a shattered economy. But, with subsequent material and technical aid from the USSR and some of its East European satellites, the Chinese succeeded in reestablishing the Northeast as China's major industrial center.

In the early years, recovery was reported by the Communists to have been rapid. Up until 1951, the task had involved simply restoration and reconstruction of the former industrial base. In 1951, the Chinese began, in addition to undertaking further large-scale restoration and reconstruction, planning new enterprises. However, in spite of Communist claims to the contrary, it is doubtful that by 1953 the Communists had restored Manchuria's industry to its pre-1945 level. Published Communist data of the period seem inflated beyond all credence.

From the Communist point of view, the overwhelming industrial concentration in the Northeast was irrational and with the First Five Year Plan (1953-57), Peking set about creating new manufacturing centers elsewhere in order to lessen the relative importance of the former. Consequently, this effort has involved mainly the expansion of old plant capacity in the Northeast and little new construction. With the emphasis on heavy industry, the Anshan Iron and Steel Works, the heart of the complex, have been restored and expanded (Map 6). In 1958, it is reported, Anshan produced 4.5 million tons of steel as compared with a peak output of half a million tons under the Japanese. Similarly, expansion of the Penki Iron and Steel Works has occurred while a new plant has been started at Fushun. Mukden continues as the major center for the manufacturing of machinery of all types. However, at Harbin in the north, new construction has given that city more weight in the industrial structure of the Northeast than it previously possessed. At least five new plants were established there with Soviet aid during the First Five Year Plan. It is a major center for the production of equipment for the electric power industry, which will undoubtedly contribute to the proposed joint Sino-Soviet development of the water resources of the Amur Basin.

The major industrial region, the Northeast, is still essentially agricultural. While it is a land of large cities (Table V), four-fifths of its population live on farms. Manchuria's millions of acres of fertile black soil yield large harvests of soybeans, kaoliang, millet, and wheat.

Table V *Population of Major Cities of Manchuria*
(1957 estimate)

Anshan, Liaoning	805,000	
Antung, Liaoning	360,000	(1953 census)
Changchun, Kirin	975,000	
Chinchow, Liaoning	352,000	(1953 census)
Fushun, Liaoning	985,000	
Harbin, Heilungkiang	1,552,000	
Kirin, Kirin	568,000	
Penki, Liaoning	449,000	(1953 census)
Tsitsihar, Heilungkiang	668,000	

Source: *Encyclopaedia Britannica World Atlas,* Chicago, 1961, p. 153.

The Japanese evacuation and civil war had had a serious effect on Manchuria's agriculture. Yet, recovery was also rather rapid. While in 1948 grain production was only 12.8 million tons as compared with 18.3 million in 1943, by 1951 it had risen substantially, though still falling short of the pre-war level. Nevertheless, large quantities of grain were shipped regularly from the Northeast into North China to feed the millions there. In the meantime, a sweeping land reform liquidated landlord holdings, which, according to Communist sources, had involved 80 per cent of the land in the hands of only 10 per cent of the farm population.[4]

The collectivization of agriculture began in China after 1951. As the Human Relations Area Files China Handbook notes, "the path of collectivization was marked by several distinct stages from mutual-aid teams through agricultural producers' cooperatives to collective farms, and finally to communes."[5] At the same time, large state farms, after the Soviet model, have been set up largely in areas where reclamation is necessary. This has been the case in northern Heilungkiang, along the Amur and Sungari Rivers, which has attracted new settlers. In 1955, Heilungkiang had 32 mechanized state farms.

Should the Amur Basin development scheme materialize, the industry and agriculture of the Northeast should benefit appreciably. The agreement between Moscow and Peking, signed in 1956, calls for the construction of a series of hydroelectric installations along the Amur and its tributaries, with a combined capacity of 13 million KW, "sufficient to meet the expected needs of industry, agriculture, and transportation." One Soviet writer has referred to the proposed program in terms of a "fourth metallurgical base in the Aldan-Amur region of Eastern Siberia." Others have stressed the extent to which such cities as Harbin, Mukden, and even Peking, will benefit from new sources of power. Improvements in the river system, too, will permit control of the seasonal flow, and eliminate the serious flooding that now occurs, thus creating more favorable conditions for agricultural development on both sides of the river.

In Sinkiang, industrialization has made some progress, but by western standards, it cannot be considered impressive. Undoubtedly, distance from China Proper and the lack of adequate (to date) transportation facilities, as well as a scarcity of trained or skilled labor, have remained obvious handicaps.

In the early years of Communist control in Sinkiang, considerable use was made of the military. In December, 1949, a decree of the

[4] O. Edmund Clubb, *Chinese Communist Development Programs in Manchuria*, New York: Institute of Pacific Relations, 1954, p. 14.

[5] Hsiao Hsia (ed.), *China: Its People, Its Society, Its Culture*, New Haven: HRAF Press, 1960, p. 340.

People's Military Revolutionary Council called on the Liberation Army to turn to economic construction. Of the 193,000 soldiers stationed there, reportedly 110,000 were assigned to work in industry and agriculture.

One of the most important tasks to be undertaken involved the construction of a railway to link the remote region to central China. In 1952, work on the Lanchow-Sinkiang Railway was begun. By mid-1960, the track had been laid to within 200 miles of Urumchi, and by mid-1961 it may have been almost completed, despite reports of a lack of steel for rails. From Urumchi, it is planned to extend the line westward past the oilfields at Tushantzu, into the Dzhungarian Gate. At the Sino-Soviet border, it will connect with the Soviet line, built in 1958 eastward from Aktogai on the Turk-Sib Railway. When completed, the Lanchow-Sinkiang Railway will constitute a vital part of a Eurasian transcontinental line, making direct rail travel possible from East Berlin to Hanoi.[6]

Other rail lines have been planned in Sinkiang, extending northward across Dzhungaria and southward into the Tarim Basin. In mid-1958, surveying began for a Kashgar-Turfan route, which would link both sides of the Tien Shan. Ultimately, too, Sinkiang is to be joined by rail to Tibet. Simultaneously with the planning of railways, a network of motor highways is being developed throughout the region. And we have already seen that strategic roads have been extended southward from Kashgar into the Karakorum Ranges, and across Outer Ladakh into the Tibetan Autonomous Region. Air transportation across the territory has been established on a regular basis, as a result of the 1950 agreement between Stalin and Mao. And, reportedly, plans have been drafted by Kazakh scientists for the construction of a 620-mile waterway linking the Ili, Chu, and Syr-Darya Rivers, thus affording Sinkiang a connection by water with the Aral Sea. Another Soviet report also emphasizes that northwestern Sinkiang has now an outlet to the Arctic Ocean, due to recent Soviet developments along the Upper Irtysh.

Sinkiang is rich in resources. The largest deposits of oil in China

[6] A. R. Field, "Strategic Development in Sinkiang," *Foreign Affairs*, January, 1961, p. 315.

lie within the region, principally at Tushantzu and Karamai. In 1953, with Soviet help, a refinery was constructed at Tushantzu. Karamai is said to be so rich, that one well alone produced 30,000 tons of oil in 1959. From Karamai a pipeline has been laid to the Tushantzu refinery.

New discoveries of coal have raised the estimated reserves to 35 billion tons, of which in 1958, 3.6 million tons were mined. Coal occurs in many places in Sinkiang, particularly near Chuguchak on the Soviet border, at Hami and near Urumchi. Iron ore, too, is found in large quantities; however, this ore does not seem to have a high iron content. At any rate, it is reported that low quality ores and poor coking coal have slowed the production of steel at the August 1st Iron and Steel Plant (built in 1951) at Urumchi. This handicap in turn has, presumably, delayed the laying of track on the Lanchow-Sinkiang Railway.

Urumchi seems destined to be the manufacturing center of the Northwest. Already it has a small diversified base, which will be assisted materially by improved transportation lines.

It may be expected, however, that the Chinese Communists will give increasing attention to the industrialization of Sinkiang. Not only is industrial development the key to transforming backward minorities into modern nations, but the Chinese have also recognized and affirmed that Sinkiang has all the material prerequisites for becoming a major industrial region of China. In 1959, for example, the Sinkiang Party Committee adopted a resolution to turn the province into a base for the production of iron and steel, petroleum, coal, nonferrous metals, cotton and other textiles, sugar and other products. And, to overcome the shortage of labor there, workers from the central provinces of China have been transported westward.

The impact of collectivization has brought about a social revolution in the countryside. In this task, the Liberation Army played a major role. This upheaval involved, first of all, confiscation of landlord holdings, redistribution of the lands, and then subsequently the formation of agricultural cooperatives. From 1950 to 1954, army farms were established, later to be reorganized into military cooperatives. Late in 1954, those units engaged in economic construction were united in a special "production-construction army," and also put to work in industry. By the spring of 1956, agriculture had been so revolutionized, that cooperatives were established throughout the Tarim Basin, where 80 per cent of the peasant holdings were concentrated. The speed with which the transformation occurred may be realized from the following figures. Whereas in 1954, there were only 147 agricultural production cooperatives in Sinkiang, by July, 1956, there were altogether 10,781. Since 1958, communes have been established in the oases.

Not only have the sedentary peoples of Sinkiang been affected by the revolution, but the nomadic tribes have also been forced to modify their traditional patterns of making a livelihood. As in the USSR and in the MPR, the Kazakh and Mongol pastoralists have been settled onto large livestock farms. At the beginning of 1957, there were 629 pastoral producers cooperatives, involving 24 per cent of all herdsmen households. Since then, communes have been established in the pastoral areas, a development which caused some Sinkiang Kazakhs to migrate into the Soviet Union, where the regime seemed less oppressive. Such pressure, undoubtedly, has forced the traditional felt yurt to yield to the "more progressive" mud or wooden house, which presumably will precede the three- or four-story stucco tenement, common throughout the Communist world.

In order to raise crop production in Sinkiang beyond the subsistence level, new areas have been brought under cultivation. Improved and extended irrigation systems are under construction, both in the Tarim oases, as well as in Dzhungaria, particularly along the Manass River. Composite expeditions of Soviet and Chinese scientists have been engaged in assessing irrigation potentials. Some of the new land will be used to produce food; the rest will go into cotton, Sinkiang's leading commercial crop.

Elsewhere, along the southern borders of the MPR, the face of the land is being changed. In Kansu, a refinery has been built to process the oil at Yumen, while a pipeline has been laid to Lanchow, where other refineries are scheduled to be put up.

In southeastern Inner Mongolia, as part of the plan to develop the industrial strength of the Northern Region, centered on Peking, an iron and steel plant is nearing completion at Paotow. When in operation (1962), it will have a steel capacity of one million tons. In Kalgan and other nearby cities, new manufacturing establishments have been built to produce mining equipment, textile machinery and trucks. On the edge of the Gobi are reportedly reclamation projects involving millions of acres of land, including the planting of extensive areas of forest shelter belts.

The industrialization and Sinification of Inner Mongolia is being aided by new railways. In 1956, a rail line was opened between Ulan Bator and Chining, thus linking Peking to the Trans-Siberian Railway across Inner and Outer Mongolia. And, from Paotow to Lanchow, paralleling the Hwang-Ho, another line has been under construction in recent years and may already have been completed.

RECENT DEVELOPMENTS IN THE MONGOLIAN PEOPLE'S REPUBLIC

Prior to 1945, when the MPR, isolated and cut off from the rest of the world, suffered under total Soviet domination, the Mongol economy made little progress toward providing a richer material life for the Mongol people. While the sown area of the republic increased substantially during the war years, primarily as a result of Soviet inability to meet the basic grain needs of the Mongols, acreage again fell to near the prewar level in the immediate postwar period. Indeed, since there had been no industrial construction to speak of during the war, postwar Mongolia differed little from the prewar period. The population had remained relatively stable at between 900,000 and a million, given an over-all density of two persons per square mile, with livestock outnumbering the Mongols by three to one (Table VI).

Table VI   *Livestock in the Mongolian People's Republic*
(1958 estimate)

Camels	864,000
Cattle	1,954,800
Goats	5,594,200
Horses	2,449,300
Sheep	12,579,900

Source: *Encyclopaedia Britannica World Atlas,* Chicago, 1961, p. 175.

The Communist success in China, however, dramatically changed the situation for Mongolia. The MPR no longer constituted a buffer between the USSR and Nationalist China, or a shield against attack on the USSR by Japan. Now Communist Mongolia, recognized as independent in 1950 by the Chinese Communists, became a territorial link between Moscow and Peking, joined by a common ideology.

Before the war the Soviet Union had been extremely niggardly in its assistance to Mongolia, probably because the Soviets could ill afford to give much, while Mongolia itself was remote, exposed, and difficult to defend in case of war. For their part, the Mongols were incapable, through lack of trained labor and of other resources, of carrying out their own development program. However, in 1946, a beginning was made at speeding up growth, assisted to a considerable degree by the Soviet Union. To a new ten-year treaty of friendship and mutual assistance with the MPR, there were added supplementary economic and cultural agreements. To improve communications a railroad was constructed south from Ulan-Ude on the Trans-Siberian to Ulan-Bator, the capital of the Mongolian Republic. The ensuing five-year plan, 1948-52, brought with it some increase in agricultural production and a start in the modernization of the capital.

The next five-year plan, 1953-57, witnessed a speed-up in development, especially as Chinese Communist assistance was now made available. In 1952, the CPR and the MPR signed a ten-year agreement for cultural and economic cooperation, while in 1955, arrangements were made whereby Chinese labor could migrate under contract to Mongolia. A number of industrial enterprises were planned under the terms of these agreements, including the construction of a large woolen textile combine. The combine, built by Chinese labor to specifications drafted by Soviet engineers with machinery purchased from Great Britain, has since been put into operation. Additional agreements with the CPR on free aid and long-term credits were reached in 1956 and in 1958, while in 1957, the USSR undertook to aid Mongolia's three-year plan (1957-60) by extending new credits.

In 1954-55, the Mongol government embarked on another major

effort to collectivize the livestock economy—this time with obviously more success. Before the end of 1959, it reported, the whole herding population of about 650,000 had joined rural economy cooperatives, while about three-fourths of the country's livestock had been collectivized.[6] Another effort, too, was made to plough up the land, relying on the lead, perhaps, of the Khrushchev virgin and idle lands program, instituted in the spring of 1954. The Mongolian program, however, was nowhere near the proportions of the Soviet, which involved the ploughing of more than 70 million acres of land. The turning of the Mongol sod got off to a slow start, but further assistance rendered by the Soviets in a treaty in 1959 sped up the development. Under this agreement the Soviet Union supplied the Mongolian grain farms with caterpillar and other tractors as well as other farm equipment. In addition, Mongolian farm workers received the assistance of Soviet agricultural specialists. By 1959, the sown area had increased five times over 1954 and wheat production had grown reportedly thirty-six times, but total acreage involved remains relatively small. However, it is doubtful if dry farming can be practiced to any extent in Mongolia because of the light and unreliable precipitation. Meanwhile, irrigation facilities have not yet been developed to any significant degree. Near Karakorum, west of Ulan-Bator, Chinese laborers have built new irrigation canals to divert the waters of the Orkhon River, yet Mongolia's irrigation potential remains rather low because of the nature and irregular flow of the rivers.

This massive reorganization of Mongolian agriculture required careful preparation as well as considerable financial assistance from outside. Veterinary facilities have been improved and a systematic campaign has been waged against livestock disease. In the cooperatives themselves, of which there are presently about 389, schools have been established as well as shops, cinemas and medical centers. And, the yurt, too, has begun to yield to fixed communities of wooden houses.

The yurt, a round, low felt tent, ideally suited to conditions in

[6] "Economic Advance in Mongolia," *The World Today,* Vol. 16, No. 6, June, 1960, p. 261.

Mongolia, is despised by the modern Mongol intellectual and party leader as a sign of backwardness. Nowhere is the struggle to replace the yurt with modern dwellings more apparent than in Ulan-Bator, the industrial center of the republic and only city of any size. There, with Soviet and Chinese assistance, rows of new apartments are rising along paved streets as Ulan-Bator presses toward the twentieth century. Within a few years when much of the heavy construction work has been completed, the capital will resemble most provincial Soviet cities. However, because Ulan-Bator is the chief city of Mongolia, whose independence has been recognized by East European and other Communist countries as well as by several outside the bloc, it should ultimately have an array of government and diplomatic buildings which may lessen the general monotony of scale and design. By far the most impressive foreign embassy yet established there is that of the Chinese People's Republic.

The industrial development of Ulan-Bator and the general economic growth of Mongolia have been assisted by improvements in transport. The railway linking the city to the Trans-Siberian was extended southward in 1955 to the Chinese border to connect with a Chinese line running northward from Tsining to Erhlien on the border. Tsining is several hundred miles due west of Peking. The Chinese portion of the line, from Tsining to Ehrlien, however, is of the same broad gauge as the Mongolian and Russian lines. Travelers on the railway report that the trip into Mongolia either from the USSR or from the CPR is made in broad gauge Russian cars, which are adaptable for use on the narrower Chinese gauge.[7] The extension of the route into China has obviously done much to facilitate the dispatch of Chinese aid to the Mongols. It has also encouraged the further exploitation of the coal fields south of Ulan-Bator and the oil deposits near Sayn-Shanda in the Gobi, in southern Mongolia. Finally, the through railways has truly made Mongolia a "corridor" and a link, rather than a dead-end street, with important international implications.

Within the past two years, further agreements with the USSR and

[7] Klaus Mehnert, "Die Transmongolische Bahn und das Verhältnis Peking-Moskau," *Osteuropa,* Vol. VII, December, 1957, pp. 868-69.

the CPR have ensured continued developmental progress for Mongolia. The May, 1960, Treaty of Friendship and Mutual Assistance with the CPR was accompanied by Agreements on Economic and Technical Aid and on Scientific and Technical Cooperation. Peking undertook to provide a long-term loan (1961-65) and assistance in the carrying out of new projects, including the construction of utilities and water conservancy measures. These agreements were followed in September, 1960, by another on Chinese labor in Mongolia. In the same month, the Soviets agreed also to provide additional aid and in December they reached a new trade arrangement with Mongolia. Subsequently, in April, 1961, the USSR promised economic assistance to Mongolia's new five-year plan and this was followed a week later by a new Chinese-Mongolian commercial treaty.

Mongolia's economic and cultural contacts are not confined to the USSR and the CPR only. The Czechs have rendered assistance in the establishment of a Mongolian shoe industry; the Hungarians have sunk wells; the East Germans have provided a color printing works; and Bulgaria has given agricultural assistance.

Thus, Communist Mongolia, bounded by the USSR and the CPR, has begun to emerge as a young, semi-modern country eager to play a more active role in the world. What its people—and its party—desire most of all, however, is recognition by the West and a place in the United Nations. Because of the opportunities, which its unique geographical position affords for observing the day to day relations between Soviet and Chinese Communist officials, United States recognition may soon be forthcoming now that the MPR has been admitted to the U.N.

IV   *The Borderlands in Sino-Soviet Relations*

THE Chinese Communist Party, founded some forty years ago, was organized with support from the Communist Party of the Soviet Union. In the early years of the party's history, there were miscalculations in tactics, some of which may be traced to Stalin. The net result was that the Chinese Communists were banished to the countryside by the Nationalists after 1927. There they were compelled to work out a new strategy for revolution, under the leadership of Mao Tse-tung. They did not, however, disavow their ideological roots and ancestors. Nor did they deny the heritage of Lenin and Stalin, or their indebtedness to the Russian Communist Party. In the closing days of World War II and in the months that followed, with Red Army assistance and captured Japanese and American equipment, the Chinese Communists achieved a surprisingly quick victory in Manchuria, and shortly thereafter throughout the mainland. Indeed, the speed with which the revolution was carried out in 1949 may have surprised the Soviets as much as it shook profoundly the West and especially the United States, which had looked forward to a friendly alliance with post-war Nationalist China.

Out of the Chinese revolution has emerged a new politico-geographic situation, the implications of which are still not fully understood in the West. For Russia and China enjoy an association which in itself is revolutionary. Linked by a common ideology, they share above all the goal of world communism to and on which all other objectives are subordinate and dependent. Yet the close state relationship, or as some western observers have termed it, the axis partnership, that has emerged between Russia and China is a contradiction of the historical record. The story of Russo-Chinese relations before 1949, particularly with respect to and as demonstrated in the borderlands, was one of traditional fear and suspicion, if not outright dislike between the peoples of either country.

Though the Ch'ing emperors were overlords of Manchuria, Outer and Inner Mongolia, much of Turkestan, and of Tibet, they were never able to effectively administer and to incorporate these territories into China. With the exception of Manchuria, and to a lesser extent, Inner Mongolia, the border regions remained non-Chinese. And, in spite of the Sinification of Manchuria, and again to a lesser degree, Inner Mongolia, foreign influence there was often more decisive than was Chinese. This situation was equally true of Sinkiang.

As we have seen, the building of the Chinese Eastern Railway at the turn of the century gave the Russians a preeminent position throughout northern and central Manchuria. Following the Russo-Japanese War in 1904, Japanese influence was on the ascendancy, although by mutual agreement spheres of interest were created within the rich province. Thirteen years later, the Bolshevik Revolution in Russia gave further stimulus to Japan's ambitions in East Asia, which reached their apogee in the 1930's, when Manchuria, as Manchukuo, functioned as a Japanese puppet state. At the same time, Japanese interest and influence in Inner Mongolia further weakened whatever remained of Chinese control of the Gobi, following the establishment, over a decade before, of an autonomous Mongolian People's Republic to the north. In Sinkiang, Russian economic penetration both before and after 1917 did not lead to the political detachment of the province from the Chinese state, but the influence of the central government of China was negligible. When the Chinese Nationalists were at last in a position to direct the administration of Sinkiang, after the Soviets were compelled to withdraw because of the war in Europe, they were unable to accomplish much. Their efforts were hampered by internal disorders in the province, and by the struggle in the east against Japan, and later, the Chinese Communists.

Now, the common ideology of Russian and Chinese Communism

has brought a stability to the borderlands that hitherto has not existed. If a final frontier between Russia and China has been found, it has emerged as a result of the combined Bolshevik and Chinese Communist Revolutions. Consequently, whatever boundary discrepancies occur on contemporary Sino-Soviet maps, in the Pamirs, along the Argun, or at the junction of the Amur-Ussuri Rivers, may not be deemed significant. At any rate, the goals of international communism outweigh the importance of any national cartographic disagreement. Indeed, nowhere do the Russians or Chinese even refer to any boundary problem between their respective countries. For the same reason, the Chinese Communists have relinquished the Nationalist Chinese claim to the historic sixty-four settlements near the mouth of the Zeya on the right bank of the Amur. While it is conceivable that adjustments may be made in the Pamirs, the present Sino-Soviet boundary must be considered a stable one, and in all probability, a final one.

Right up until the Communist success in Manchuria and the takeover in Sinkiang, the Soviets had hoped to make these two strategic territories dependent on—if not an outright part of—the Soviet Union. This strategy may account for the systematic stripping of Manchurian industry. It may also help to explain why the Soviets continued to maneuver in Sinkiang, while the Nationalists were preoccupied with the Communists elsewhere. At any rate, the victory of Communism in China compelled a reassessment of Soviet policy. The withdrawal of the Soviets from Manchuria and Sinkiang was not immediate, but in one way or another, it came within five years. Whatever the reasons for the delay, it is of major significance that the Soviets did withdraw. The surrender was unprecedented in Russian history, not only because they gave up an area to which they had long had a vital interest, but they did so voluntarily. But it was a surrender, not to Nationalist China, to Japan, or to any other "capitalistic" country; it was a surrender to Communist China, to comrades in the international struggle. Since then, of course, the Chinese Communists have taken major steps to integrate and to ensure wherever necessary the ultimate Sinification of the Chinese borderlands.

Consequently then, if the ideological solidarity between Russia and China is accepted as a basic premise, the Russian Communists cannot be concerned about the restoration and development of industry by the Chinese in Manchuria; they cannot consider Manchuria in Communist Chinese hands a threat to the sparsely-settled, undeveloped lands east of Lake Baikal in Siberia. While the current Soviet Seven-Year Plan envisages further industrialization in Siberia, and simultaneously a substantial increase in its population, this program of development must be thought of in the context of overall Soviet growth, rather than as a response to any potential or hypothetical threat from China. Moreover, as we have already noted, there exist joint Sino-Soviet plans for the development of the water resources of the Amur Basin, which, when implemented should stimulate the economic growth of the Soviet Far East, as well as of China's North Northeast Regions.

Finally, the construction of railways linking China and Mongolia, and China and the USSR, through Sinkiang and Kazakhstan, must also be viewed in terms of the long-range Communist strategy. Some observers profess to see a danger to China in the Mongolian railway. In case of Sino-Soviet conflict, Russian-made cars could roll on the broad-gauge right into Inner Mongolia, whereas standard-gauge Chinese cars could not move past Tsining. The Lanchow-Sinkiang line, however, will be standard-gauge, meeting at the Soviet border the broad-gauge Aktogai line. If one assumes that the relationship between the two giant states, supported by the ideological ties of their respective Communist Parties, is to be an enduring one, then the construction of the railways, wide-gauge notwithstanding, will assuredly be of great value to the CPR. Not only do they bring the CPR closer to the MPR, but they also make possible the economic development of the rich resources of Sinkiang, not to mention the role they should play in overall development of the vast heartland of Asia, whether Russian, Chinese—or Mongolian.

In Sinkiang, as in Manchuria, the Soviets have provided economic assistance to the Chinese Communists. In spite of historical Russian concern over the Inner Asian gateways, and Soviet interest in the mineral resources of the area, Sinkiang is now accepted as Chinese. The native Uighurs, Kazakhs, and Mongols will be Sinified, but they will also be Communized. The end result will be a weakening of native cultures, as well as of the ethnic and other ties that link the minorities of Sinkiang to those of Soviet Central Asia. The Turks of Inner Asia are not to be allowed to become a great united people, nor will they be permitted to make an independent contribution to world communism; their participation will be possible only by means of the Communist Party of the Soviet Union and/or the Chinese Communist party.

A similar Sino-Soviet policy seems to prevail with respect to the Mongols. In that quarter, however, the situation is somewhat more complex, because of the existence of a third state, the Mongolian People's Republic. Though a part of the Ch'ing empire, Outer Mongolia is nevertheless recognized today by the Chinese Communists as independent. Some western observers believe that with the building of the railway, entailing financial and material aid to the MPR by Chinese Communists along with the migration of thousands of Chinese workmen, would jeopardize Russian hegemony in that area. Indeed, a visit to the Chinese embassy building in Ulan Bator, which is considerably more elaborate than that of the Soviets, might leave one with the distinct impression that the Chinese Communists have outdone themselves, particularly as Ulan Bator can make no claim to being the influential capital of a country of international import. Nevertheless, there is no concrete or satisfactory evidence to suggest that the Chinese Communists are attempting or planning to challenge the Soviets in Mongolia. All that may be claimed is that Chinese influence in the republic is unquestionably on the rise, *and* on the surface, at least, Mongolia stands to benefit; *but* the MPR remains oriented politically toward Moscow. Moreover, it is noteworthy that in Mongolia, efforts are being made to promote ties and to strengthen the friendship between the Mongols and Chinese on the one hand, as well as between the Mongols and the Russians on the other. Meanwhile, although the Outer Mongols continue justifiably proud of the exploits of the great 13th-century Mongol leader, Genghis Khan, there is no indication that they may harbor pan-Mongolist feelings.

At any rate, it would seem that the Mongol peoples as a whole— the Outer Mongols, the Inner Mongols of China, and the Buriats of the USSR—are to remain divided, while the historic cultural links between them are to be further weakened. The Latinization of the Inner Mongol alphabet will establish a barrier to literary communication with the Outer Mongols, who have adopted the Cyrillic alphabet. Increasing Sinification of the Inner Mongols will cause yet greater modification of age-old customs. On the other hand, the Buriat Mongols of Siberia have, for three hundred years, been under Russian domination, and Russification and Sovietization have made considerable progress. Indeed, some Buriat scholars, whom this author has met, seem more at home in the Russian language than in the language of their ancestors. Consequently, divided and weakened, the Mongol peoples, numbering over two and a half million in East Asia, cannot speak with one voice. The Outer Mongols may be allowed to speak for the MPR, especially in world councils, but even that privilege may be more hypothetical than real.

It is believed by some observers in the West that conflict between the USSR and the CPR is inevitable—would be inevitable regardless of politics—because of China's demographic problem. [No one knows for certain how large the mainland Chinese population is, but it possibly totals well above 600 million, and is increasing anywhere from 10 to 15 million per year.] Wilhelm Starlinger, a German doctor who spent five years in a Soviet concentration camp, emerged in 1953 convinced that China would be compelled to find a solution to its rapidly growing population by moving into Trans-Baikalia and the Soviet Far East, and into Outer Mongolia, as well as into southeast Asia.[1]

Starlinger's conclusions were based on very superficial evidence, but nevertheless they have had considerable impact on geopolitical

---

[1] John E. Tashjean, *Where China Meets Russia: An Analysis of Dr. Starlinger's Theory.* Central Asian Collectanea, No. 2, Washington, D.C., 67 pp.

thinking in both France and West Germany. While Soviet territory east of Lake Baikal is sparsely occupied, its population-carrying capacity—especially in terms of agriculture—is not great. Undoubtedly, greater densities could be achieved, perhaps through further industrialization, but crop cultivation suffers severe handicaps due to the short growing season and permafrost. Nor is it conceivable that high, dry Mongolia, where the irrigation potential is relatively low, could support a sizeable increase in population that might be sufficient to ease in any way the congestion in China Proper. On the other hand, further development in northern Manchuria is possible, where it is estimated that up to 30 million acres may be brought into cultivation in part through drainage and other reclamation projects. But a one-year increase in China's population would, if transplanted to northern Manchuria, still not solve the overall problem.

Mr. Harrison Salisbury, a correspondent for *The New York Times,* formerly stationed in Moscow, and a more acute observer of Soviet and Chinese affairs than was Dr. Starlinger, also sees the possibility of Sino-Soviet conflict. "For it is perfectly apparent," Salisbury writes, "to anyone who reads the statistics (i.e., of China's population growth), that (there) . . . are going to be heavy and continuous population pressures on those great vacant lands of Russia's to the East (lands, incidentally, which in most cases were at one time the property of China) . . ." [2] Salisbury also attributes the Khrushchev virgin and idle lands program which in 1954-56, resulted, in the ploughing of millions of acres of unused land in western Siberia and northern Kazakhstan—and the settling of several hundred thousand Russians and Ukrainians there, as proof of Soviet concern for its vast empty Siberian spaces. The Khrushchev program unquestionably has political overtones, but more compelling reasons for its implementation may be found in domestic conditions in the Soviet Union, than in the Chinese population problem.

The official Communist line with respect to population has been that overpopulation is a myth generated by Malthusian reactionaries

[2] Harrison E. Salisbury, *To Moscow—and Beyond,* New York: Harper & Bros., 1959, p. 249.

to conceal the true cause of human misery—capitalism.[3] As Friedrich Engels stated: "If Malthus had not considered the matter so one-sidedly, he could not have failed to see that surplus population or labor power is invariably tied up with surplus wealth, surplus capital, and surplus landed property."[4] But, as one contemporary Chinese Communist writes: "After people have freed themselves from heavy fetters and established a socialist system, they become the masters of land and machine; pursuing self-conscious labor, instead of being compelled to work; and a large population becomes a very important factor in promoting the rapid development of the national economy and culture. Under such circumstances, the larger the population is, the greater, faster, better, and more economic will be socialist construction; the faster will a nation become rich and strong, with the people enjoying a higher level of material and cultural life."[5]

Nevertheless, in spite of this approach to population, the Chinese Communist Party newspaper, *People's Daily,* in 1957 carried an editorial on birth control.[6] Stating that China's population is increasing by more than 13 million per year, and that economic development cannot catch up with this rapid growth, the paper urged the regime to spread the use of birth control measures and to discourage early marriages.

Finally, in connection with China's demographic situation, Professor Karl Wittfogel of the University of Washington offers an interpretation, based on his very considerable knowledge of Marxism and of the historical development of both Russia and China, which takes issue with both Starlinger and Salisbury. Wittfogel points out that the thesis of neither man takes into consideration the effect of the collectivization of agriculture on the Chinese population.[7] As a result of collectivization, according to Wittfogel, China does not have

[3] Kingsley Davis, "The Political Impact of New Population Trends," *Foreign Affairs,* January, 1958, p. 293.

[4] Quoted in *Hsin Chien-she* (New Construction), No. 5, Peking, May, 1960, pp. 1-13.

[5] *Ibid.,* pp. 14-19.

[6] Davis, *op. cit.*

[7] Karl A. Wittfogel, "Demography," in *Bear and Dragon: What is the Relation Between Moscow and Peking?* ed. by James Burham, published by the National Review, Inc., New York, 1960, pp. 33-36.

a problem of surplus population, but rather suffers a shortage of labor in the countryside, which is likely to persist during the next "historical" period. Thus, rather than seeking foreign outlets for this population, the Chinese Communists will be compelled to seek a solution in increased productivity on the communes or farms.

This analysis, when viewed in the light of Soviet Russian experience however, begs the question. How do the Chinese Communists intend to raise the productivity of the countryside, where under ancient techniques of intensive cultivation, yields have traditionally been high? Because of differing man-arable land ratios, the Chinese situation is not comparable to the Soviet Russian, where total agricultural production has increased primarily through an expansion of the sown area. Since 1928, there is little evidence to support any Soviet claim to a significant increase in yields per acre on Soviet farms. In China, on the other hand, one cannot expect substantial additions to the crop land, other than in marginal areas; primarily in northern Manchuria, in Sinkiang, and in the sub-humid Chinese lands west of the coastal plains. Developmental projects on these lands—far from limitless—will entail, moreover, considerable initial investment, involving extensive drainage and/or irrigation.

In their development of the borderlands, as well as of China as a whole, the Chinese Communists need—and will probably continue to need for some time to come—Soviet aid, including materials, and technical assistance. Indeed, the relation between the two states may be looked upon as that of the more highly industrialized USSR assisting the less industrialized China, as Britain and the USA assist modern India.

But, according to western observers, China has not received the credits and loans from the Soviet Union, which they deem necessary for China's growth. On a per capita basis, China has received from the USSR since 1950 less than some of the East European satellites. Indeed, both the UAR and Iraq have been granted large Soviet loans, which are all the more significant because the republics are non-Communist. Political considerations unquestionably govern to a large extent the manner in which the Soviet Union doles out the rubles. Western observers cite the niggardly Soviet loans to China as an indication that Russia does not want to see China advance too rapidly.

As a matter of fact, the Soviet Union did not give the CPR any financial grants during the First Five-Year Plan. Moreover, of the Soviet credits and loans to the CPR, reportedly totaling $1.31 billion, only a small part is definitely known to have consisted of long-term loans for economic development.[8] Furthermore, by the end of 1957, according to one observer, "Peking had used up all past Soviet loans and credits, was paying the Russians large amounts (between $250 and $300 million annually) in servicing and repayment of past Soviet loans and credits, and thus had to support increasingly large export surpluses in its trade with the USSR.[9] Yet, without Soviet assistance, the CPR could not have implemented its First Five-Year Plan. However, it is possible that economic issues may have been—"and in the future are perhaps likely to be"—a greater problem in Sino-Soviet relations than has been apparent to date.[10] Nonetheless, one Soviet writer asserted in 1960 that "the economic relations between the USSR and the CPR are weighted in favor of China, since the Soviet Union, which was first in taking the road to socialist construction, has a more powerful economy, a more highly developed science and technology, and greater experience in the construction of socialism. On the other hand, as it implements effective socialist reorganization and a rapid development of the economy of the country, the CPR gives ever greater help to the Soviet Union by sharing with it the valuable experience of many centuries . . . and by supplying the USSR with some useful minerals, various manufactures, and rare subtropical products . . . to the benefit of Communist construction in our country." [11]

Since the Soviet loans to China are apart from other help rendered, such as technical assistance and technical training of per-

[8] Robert C. North, "The Sino-Soviet Alliance," *The China Quarterly,* No. 1, Jan.-Mar., 1960, p. 56.

[9] *Ibid.,* quoting A. Doak Bennett, *Communist Economic Strategy: The Rise of Mainland China,* New York: National Planning Association, 1959, p. 80.

[10] North, *loc. cit.*

[11] M. I. Sladkovskii, "Sovetsko-kitaiskoe ekonomicheskoe sotrudnicheskoe," *Problemy vostokovedeniia,* No. 3, July, 1960, pp. 108-117.

sonnel, it is impossible at this time to assess fully the Soviet contribution. Until this can be done we may consider such Soviet statements as the one cited above propagandistic, and western comments on the matter, to some extent, speculative.

The Treaty of Friendship, Alliance, and Mutual Assistance between the USSR and the CPR, signed in 1950, is the instrument for achieving the ultimate goal of international communism. China is not strong enough to play a fully independent role in world affairs, and must rely on Soviet friendship and assistance, economic or otherwise. Without the Chinese alliance, the USSR, too, would be considerably weakened. Together the USSR and the CPR present a formidable line-up, and a most serious challenge to the western and other democratic countries. Never before in history has the free world faced such a threat, and never before have the consequences of a world war appeared more horrifying. Hence, anything that could weaken or tear apart the Russo-Chinese axis would seem to benefit the West.

In the latter part of 1959 and throughout 1960, as a result of different views expressed in statements issued in Peking and Moscow, the notion of a possible falling out between the two powers gained considerable momentum in some western capitals. The desire to see a conflict develop between the CPR and the USSR is a legitimate one, but it may tend to blind the West to fundamental realities if undue weight is given to seemingly apparent signs of rift, when in fact nothing of a fundamental nature may exist.

However, the Khrushchev de-Stalinization program, later followed by his criticism of Communist Chinese efforts to force the peasantry into communes, compelled the Chinese to make clear that China "was not obliged to follow in the footsteps of the Russians." [12] Mao, unlike the chief contenders for power in the USSR, successfully carried through a revolution after a long period of experience in the countryside, fashioning a party and an elite. On the other hand, the Chinese reportedly are critical of Khrushchev for his willingness to sit down and discuss international problems with the West. The Soviet position in recent years has been that revolution is not for

[12] North, *op. cit.*, p. 58.

export, and that military action is to be avoided as a means of ex-
panding the Communist sphere.[13] War between the socialist camp
and the "imperialist" countries is no longer inevitable, because of the
holocaust that atomic weapons would rain down on everyone—including the socialist countries. To the "orthodox" Chinese Communists, this thinking is "revisionist." So long as capitalist countries
remain, the class struggle will go on, and intervention—which need
not lead to world conflict—is necessary in order to intensify the
struggle.

Recently, however, the Soviets have attempted to weaken the
basis of the reports of a sharpening ideological dispute between the
Parties of the two countries. And the Chinese Communists, too, have
denounced "the gossip" circulating in the Western press and em-
bassies about Sino-Soviet relations.[14]

As China develops industrially, adjustments will undoubtedly have
to be made within the Communist orbit, so that the Chinese Communists may play a more active role and make a greater contribution
to the overall goal. But, in the West, it must be remembered that the
leaders of the two countries differ not in terms of their objective, but
rather over the strategy and methods of achieving the objective. As
one writer points out, "It may seem paradoxical to state the truth
that *the leaders of China and Russia differ not in matters that divide
them, but in matters that unite them.*"[15] In Mao Tse-tung's words,
the differences between China and the Soviet Union are "non-
antagonistic; and such differences not only do not hinder cooperation, but, on the contrary, stimulate progress."[16]

So long as the ideological solidarity of the Parties is maintained,
there can be no break between the USSR and the CPR, even though
controversy may extend over a host of problems. "The Communist'
Parties must work for a united front of 'all democratic and patriotic'

---

[13] "Moscow and Peking Agree to Differ," *The World Today*, Vol. 17, No.
2, Feb., 1961, pp. 68-76. See also A. N. Halpern, "Communist China and
Peaceful Co-existence," *The China Quarterly*, No. 3, July-Sept., 1960, pp. 16-31.
   [14] *The New York Times*, July 9, 1961.
   [15] Wlodzimierz Baczkowski, "World History," in *Bear and Dragon*, pp. 9-13.
   [16] *Ibid.*

forces against U.S. imperialism and its allies, in order to safeguard peace." [17] In the light of this overriding unity, the historic problem of the Russo-Chinese borderlands would seem at last to have been settled.

[17] *The World Today, op. cit.,* p. 74.

V *A Political-Geographical Assessment*

TODAY, the Eurasian landmass from East Berlin to Hanoi lies within the grip of Communism. Within this vast extent of territory, the pre-eminent political unit is the USSR. Industrially, the Soviet Union is the most highly developed, and its science and military armament the most advanced. It is, above all, the oldest Communist state and the citadel of Communist ideology and power. But the emergence of Communism in China, "the land of 600 million," requires that we give attention to the CPR, if only because of its present sheer weight of numbers. Mao Tse-tung is a successful revolutionary, and this fact alone will ensure for China a voice in determining Communist strategy. And as the industrial strength of the CPR grows and as science enhances the country's military effectiveness, the Chinese will in future doubtlessly make a greater contribution to total Communist power. While there are, reportedly, differences of opinion within and between the Communist parties of the USSR and the CPR on methods to be used in the struggle with the West, yet the solidarity between the two states will in all probability remain firm. Certainly, the CPR will be in no position to challenge Soviet leadership of the bloc—or even to play a role independent of the USSR—for many decades to come. In the meantime, the immediate objective of the Communists is the steady development of the territories under their control, including the valuable lands that lie between Russia and China Proper.

The relationship between the USSR and the CPR is obviously one that, because of the multiplicity and complexity of the factors involved, is exceedingly difficult for Westerners to comprehend. Some observers in the West refer to it, in rather conventional terms, as the

Moscow-Peking Axis,[1] which of course immediately brings to mind another partnership of two decades ago, between Nazi Germany and Fascist Italy. However, according to Professor Donald Treadgold of the University of Washington, the parallel does not reflect comparable situations. "It is not at all clear," he writes, "that the Communist totalitarian states, wherein terror is a fundamental ingredient of governmental practice and wherein the ruling agency is, at least overtly, a monolithic international movement, the Communist Party, ought to be considered as essentially similar in structure and behavior to nation states, as nineteenth- and early twentieth-century international relations conceived them. Of course the external structure of nationhood remains, and is useful to the Communists in that part of their activities whereby they attempt to operate within recognized and accepted international organizations and relationships . . ."[2] However, it is not necessary, he believes, to state that the older idea of "nation" may be irrelevant in examining the USSR and the CPR, but only that it is insufficient, "to explain either the domestic policies and practices of Communist governments . . . or the expansion of the international Communist movement beyond Communist-ruled countries . . .

"Communists use nationalism, as they use other devices or ideas or institutions in which they discern instrumental value at a given moment. They may also, more or less unwittingly, be used by nationalism, but it seems clear that their unconscious motivation has been very much less related to love of nation than to desire for power—not the whimsical arbitrariness of the Oriental despot, or the institutionally unrestrained (though often limited legally) prerogatives of the Western absolutist monarch, but of power without limit; power not only to kill a man but to extinguish his memory, power not only to change human institutions but the nature of man itself, power such as that to which seldom any sane man and never any significant political movement has before aspired . . ."

[1] Howard L. Boorman and others, *Moscow-Peking Axis: Strengths and Strains,* New York: Harper & Bros., 1957, 227 pp.

[2] Donald W. Treadgold, "Russia and the Far East," an essay to appear in a volume to be published by Yale University Press, 1962.

Any attempt at understanding the present political-geographical structure in Eurasia must take into consideration the factors mentioned above. This is especially true if one is to examine the Communist power bloc in the light of the writings and prognostications of the late British geographer, Sir Halford Mackinder, as many geographers are inclined to do. For the first time in modern history, much of Eurasia is united and dominated by forces inherently hostile to the West. Mackinder, writing in the period from 1904 to 1942, did not foresee the present alignment, which would place the heart of the Eurasian landmass in the hands of a strong power or of strong powers linked by treaty or ideology. But he was very much concerned that control of the area would afford the possessor enormous advantages, which might lead to world domination.

In 1904, when Mackinder first spoke of the problem,[3] the Eurasia that had lain open to the horse-riding nomads of antiquity was about to be crossed by rail and brought under effective organization. "There have been, and are here," he stated, "the conditions for a mobility of military and economic power of a far-reaching yet limited character." This vast internal region, with its great potential, he called the Pivot Area. Its boundary extended southward from the Arctic Ocean east of Arkhangel, through central European Russia into the Caucasus Mountains. From the Caucasus, passing to the southwest of the Caspian Sea, the boundary cut across the southern part of the Iranian or Persian plateau, and northward across Afghanistan and what is now West Pakistan to the lofty Karakorum Mountains. To the east and northeast, it proceeded through Tibet, the Kansu Corridor, and eastern Mongolia. Skirting on the west the Amur Basin, the boundary again reached the Arctic Ocean near the mouth of the Kolyma River in eastern Siberia. The Pivot Area, accordingly, included the northern and interior portion of the Eurasian mass, where the rivers flowed either into the ice-blocked Arctic or into land-locked interior basins. Thus the pivot was inaccessible to the sea, and free of any threat from a hostile power whose striking force was based solely on the sea. Whoever occupied

[3] H. S. Mackinder, "The Geographical Pivot of History," *Geographical Journal,* Vol. 23, 1904, pp. 421-431.

the central, strategic position could strike on all sides and be struck from all sides, save on the north. As Mackinder indicated, the full development of railways in the pivot would permit the mobility necessary for the development of the territory's resources as well as affording the means of defense on all sides and the ability to strike out on all sides.

In 1904, Tsarist Russia controlled politically much of the pivot. *It was a raw, undeveloped land.* Railways had been built or were being built southward from Moscow and into the Caucasus, into and through Russian Turkestan—only recently incorporated into the empire—as well as through the Urals and across Siberia to the Pacific.

In those parts of the Pivot Area that lay outside tsarist control, the Russians had established spheres of influence or indicated a strong interest in doing so. This situation was true of Persia, Afghanistan, and Tibet, where the British in India presented an opposing force; it was also true of Sinkiang and Mongolia, which were part of the declining Ch'ing empire. Throughout the latter 19th and early 20th centuries, as was noted in an earlier chapter, these regions, peripheral to the Russian empire but within the Pivot Area, were zones of tension and remained as such until almost the eve of World War I.

Surrounding the Pivot Area were the Crescent Areas: an Inner Crescent, partly continental and partly oceanic, and an Outer Crescent, wholly oceanic. The Inner Crescent included those territories, immediately beyond the Pivot, which extended from Scandinavia through Europe, North Africa, and the Middle East, into the peninsulas of South and East Asia. The pivot power, Russia, created additional zones of tension, by seeking to extend further its influence in parts of the Inner Crescent, notably in the Balkans, the Middle East, North China, and Manchuria. In these areas, Russia was rather effectively checked: by the Austro-Hungarians and, to some extent, the Turks in southeastern Europe; by the British in the Middle East; and, as the Russo-Japanese War soon proved, by the Japanese in the Far East.

Beyond the Inner Crescent lay the Outer Crescent, consisting of the maritime states: Great Britain, the Americas, antipodal Africa, Australasia, and Japan, whose seats of power were wholly oceanic.

"In the present condition of the balance of power," Mackinder wrote, "Russia was not equivalent to the peripheral states. However, the oversetting of the balance of power in favor of the pivot state, resulting in its expansion over the marginal lands of Eurasia, would permit the use of vast continental resources for fleet-building, *and the empire of the world would then be in sight*. This might happen," Mackinder feared, "if Germany were to ally herself with Russia. The threat of such an event should, therefore, throw France into alliance with the over-sea powers, and France, Italy, Egypt, India, and Korea would become so many bridgeheads, where the outside navies would support armies to compel the pivot allies to deploy land forces and prevent them from concentrating their whole strength on fleets. . . ."

Mackinder in 1904 did not prophesy that Russia would one day rule the world; rather, as a geographer who had studied the course of Asian history, he believed that whatever power controlled the pivot, whether Russia allied with Germany, or a conquering China supported by Japan, would enjoy enormous geographical advantages that could lead to world empire.

In the years that followed up to the outbreak of World War I, an alignment of powers took place, but it did not create the conditions that concerned Mackinder. Rather, in fighting World War I, Russia was compelled to reach out into the Crescents for allies against Germany and the associated Austro-Hungarians, both of the Inner Crescent. Nor did conditions exist at the end of the war to promote strength in the pivot. Imperial Russia collapsed under the war effort, suffered revolution, and was shortly to be torn by civil war. Imperial Germany "lost" the war and similarly suffered revolution. In the Far East, Japan superseded Russia, while China, under the Nationalists, was undergoing its own revolution—but there was little evidence, in the light of Japan's own ambitions, of a Sino-Japanese accord, which would sweep China into control of the pivot.

In 1919, nevertheless, Mackinder saw fit to make another statement of his assessment of the Pivot Area.[4] Enlarging the pivot to include

[4] Sir Halford J. Mackinder, *Democratic Ideals and Reality. A Study in the Politics of Reconstruction,* New York: Henry Holt & Co., 1st ed. 1919, reissued 1942, 219 pp. The following discussion is based on the text.

the southwestern uplands of China and virtually all of Mongolia, he renamed it the Heartland. To this he added an East European Zone, including the basins of the Black and Baltic Seas. "Regarded from the point of view of human mobility, and of the different modes of mobility, it is evident that since land-power can today close the Black Sea, the whole basin of that sea must be regarded as of the Heartland. . . ." Furthermore, "the Baltic is a sea which can now be 'closed' by land-power." With the railway, the motor-car and the aeroplane—though, admittedly, "of a boomerang nature"—"a great military power in possession of the Heartland . . . could take easy possession of the crossways of the world . . ." Thus, for Mackinder,

> "Who rules East Europe commands the Heartland:
> Who rules the Heartland commands the World-Island:
> Who rules the World-Island commands the World."

Consequently, in 1919, Mackinder urged that East Europe be divided into a multi-state system which would shield Russia against Germany. For, Mackinder believed, "the Russians are, and for one, if not two, generations must remain, hopelessly incapable of resisting German penetration on any basis but that of a military autocracy, unless they be shielded from direct attack." The danger, therefore, lay in a resurgent Germany, with its Prussian military tradition, taking over control of East Europe, which would then open up to Germany the whole of the Heartland.

In the inter-war period, the Rappallo Agreements between Russia and Germany in 1923 and the later Nazi-Soviet Pact in 1939 might have suggested respectively that, far from Germany over-running Russia, the Germans and Russians might join together to dominate Eurasia. However, traditional antipathies, together with the over-riding mutual distrust of the Nazis and Communists, made a long-term accord impossible. World War II ensued, which in June, 1941, involved the dramatic invasion of the Soviet Union by Germany.

During the height of World War II, Mackinder restated his hypothesis.[5] The Heartland remained virtually the same, though he

[5] Sir Halford J. Mackinder, "The Round World and the Winning of the Peace," *Foreign Affairs,* July, 1943, pp. 595-605.

might have excluded the forested, mountainous territory east of the Yenisei River in Siberia, which he called Lenaland. And, noting the strength of the USSR, which included with its boundaries much of the Heartland, Mackinder pointed out that "for the first time in all history, there is within this vast natural fortress a garrison adequate to deny entry to the German invader. Given that fact . . . , the sheer breadth of the open gateway (i.e., a thousand miles wide, from peninsular Europe into the interior plain of Eurasia) is an advantage, for it provides the opportunity of defeating the enemy by compelling him to make a broad deployment of his manpower."

Following the war, the Soviet Union extended its power throughout East Europe to the banks of the Elbe and the shores of the Adriatic Sea. In Asia, as we have seen, having already established a decisive control over the Mongolian People's Republic, and having annexed Tannu Tuva, the Soviets were set to regain their position in Sinkiang and Manchuria. Indeed, in the Far East, Stalin secured for Russia, in the wartime agreements with Britain and the U.S., all that had been lost—and more—in 1905.

Mackinder, however, did not foresee the possibility of an alliance between Russia and China. Certainly, in 1943, he could not have foretold a Communist victory in China in 1949, which would establish subsequently a revolutionary political-geographical situation in Eurasia. Together, Soviet Russia and Communist China have brought under their immediate control virtually all of Mackinder's Heartland—save the Persian plateau—while Russia continues preeminent in East Europe, and China commands the Far Eastern portion of the Inner Crescent. In the light of Mackinder's strategic evaluation of the Eurasian landmass, it would seem that, under Soviet Russia and Communist China, the conditions exist which are necessary prerequisites for world empire.

Taken together, the USSR and the CPR, with their satellite territories, control approximately one billion people, and have access to incalculable resources. Development of these resources has not everywhere been the same, tending in general to diminish from west to east. The economic strength of Communist China is still in infancy as compared with that of the USSR. Yet, allowing for the influence of different historical, geographical, and demographic factors in China, one is compelled to assume that, under a program of forced industrialization, comparable to that adopted in the USSR over the last thirty years, the CPR will make important strides over the next quarter century.[6] In spite of contrary statements made in the West, there are no fully documented reasons for believing that the Soviets would not welcome and assist Chinese growth as it fits into overall strategy.

For many years to come, in spite of efforts to decentralize, the center of Chinese industrial strength will remain in the Northeast Region, or Manchuria. The wide array of industrial resources, the agricultural wealth and potential, the fine network of railways and communications, and the existing manufacturing base, with its modernized plant and trained labor supply, will ensure Manchuria a leading role in the evolution of the new China. Moreover, the joint development of the Amur Basin with the Soviets will stimulate even further growth—not only in Manchuria and North China, but also in the Soviet Far East. Up to now, in the adjoining Soviet territory, economic growth has been hampered by nature. The agricultural potential is not large, and the industrial resource base is weak. While the Soviet Far East has experienced a substantial rate of increase in its population over past decades, it remains relatively unpopulated compared with the western parts of the USSR and with Manchuria beyond the border.

Sinkiang's rich mineral resources will assist materially its industrial growth. Not only are there extensive deposits of coal, but the reserves of oil, including those of nearby Kansu as well, are the largest in China. Indeed, the oil deposits of China's Northwest are the largest yet discovered in Asia between the shores of the Caspian Sea and Sakhalin Island. While Sinkiang's present manufacturing base is not substantial by Western standards, the Chinese, with Soviet assistance, are making a prodigious effort to transform the region. Incidentally, the development and placement of industries in Sinkiang hardly bears out the predictions of conflict between the USSR and the CPR.

[6] Stefan T. Possony, "Strategy," in *Bear and Dragon*, pp. 28-32.

Indeed, the industrial decentralization that is occurring in the USSR, i.e., the emphasis currently placed on the development of the non-European parts of the Union, and the attempts of the Chinese to distribute their industry more "rationally" over the Republic, are obviously basic requirements in the nuclear age. It is apparent that the Chinese Communists are planning the development of a series of industrial islands, as far away from any sea approach as possible. Certainly, nuclear-powered Polaris submarines might find it very difficult to reach targets in the Chinese Northwest, located as it is midway between the Atlantic, the Pacific, the Arctic, and the Indian Oceans.[7]

Thus the Chinese efforts in Sinkiang, coupled with those of the Soviets in Kazakhstan, may establish a major power center in the heart of the continent. The isolation of Central Asia from United States bases, in addition to other considerations, has already helped to create ideal sites for intercontinental missiles and rockets. The first Soviet sputnik was launched from a point near the Aral Sea, and there have been unconfirmed reports of atomic explosions in Sinkiang. Finally, the further development of Inner Asian rail links between the USSR and the CPR will facilitate the movement of economic aid, as well as military equipment and supplies, to central and southern China—on lines that would be invulnerable to naval blockade, and relatively secure against airborne attack launched from bases or naval craft off the coast of China.

However, granted the rapid development of interior regions of Eurasia, does this mean today that world domination by the Communist powers is inevitable? Mackinder, as we have seen, recognized that control of the Heartland would, of necessity, give to the possessor distinct and impressive geographic advantages. But it should be noted that Mackinder's hypothesis was that of an islander, who fully understood the role that sea power played in the establishment of the British Empire. From his vantage point, he was literally overwhelmed by his *own* interpretation of the assets of the Heartland. Even allowing for the economic advance that had occurred in Siberia between 1900 and World War II, much of the territory still remained

[7] Field, *op. cit.,* p. 313. (see footnote 6, Chapter IV)

"colonial" and undeveloped, as well as difficult to reach overland. At the same time, the rest of the Heartland beyond the borders of the USSR had changed but little over the preceding half-century. Moreover, though Mackinder acknowledged that changing technology might bring forth a different assessment of geographic location and position, he did not fully comprehend the role that air transport would play, nor was he able to visualize the more recent developments in missiles and rockets.

Whether or not the Communists dominate the world may depend how effectively they are able to overcome the obvious geographic disadvantages of their vast territories. Much of central and eastern Siberia, as well as the northern half of Mongolia, are underlain with permafrost, making construction difficult in many areas, particularly in the Far North. On the other hand, much of Inner Asia, distant from the great oceans and shut off from the moisture-bearing winds by high mountains, is extremely arid. Aridity, coupled with a short growing season, adversely affects crop cultivation. Sufficient evidence is available to suggest that the Soviets, let alone the Chinese Communists, have not solved their agricultural problems. Indeed, because yields had not shown any significant increase during the years of Soviet power, the Russians embarked on their gigantic virgin and idle land scheme in 1954, in order to help improve the inadequate food base. But the more than 75 millions of acres ploughed were precisely in those regions which are frequently drought-stricken, i.e., along the lower Volga, in western Siberia, and northern Kazakhstan. It is doubtful if a similar, though substantially smaller, program in Mongolia will in any way alter the traditional livestock economy of that country. Indeed, without irrigation, one must be sceptical of Communist efforts to cultivate the drier margins of their lands, unless sound agricultural techniques are employed. Reports from the USSR indicate that in the Russian drive to raise overall production, by ploughing virgin lands, the result has been a general disregard for agricultural principles, with the result that wind erosion has been serious. It would seem that the Soviets are sacrificing long-run to short-run objectives. Yet, while the Russians have enjoyed success in the expansion of irrigation facilities in Soviet

Central Asia, it is doubtful that Sinkiang can offer the same hope to the Chinese, because of the less satisfactory water-resource base of the territory.

The enormous size of the Communist Eurasian bloc also compels the construction of long transportation lines. While the jet means that within 12 hours or less one may fly from Moscow to Peking, freight still must move over the surface. Eurasia has no navigable waterways extending from east to west for any distance, and although there are plans to divert rivers and to construct canals in western Siberia and in Inner Asia, these are in the future. Indeed, the difficulties involved in construction may make such developments too costly, or, if completed, they may not, due to the short navigation season, serve any practical purpose. Movement over the surface in the foreseeable future will have to depend on rail or highway. While a framework for rail transportation is taking shape, all-weather highways are still virtually non-existent. Thus, it cannot be said that the Communist powers, particularly throughout Inner Asia, in the lands which link Russia and China, have that mobility which Mackinder believed essential to achieving supremacy in the world. In fact, such mobility may not be achieved for many decades to come.

On the other hand, Communist domination may depend on other factors which have very little to do with location. Communism is a faith born of despair. It makes the greatest appeal to those who strive for a fuller material life—and demand it immediately. However, for the Marxists, Communism is to be ushered in only after Capitalism has been overthrown. Indeed, according to historical determinism, the next stage in man's development can only be Communism. Lenin's contribution to the dialectic involved the role of a revolutionary elite, a disciplined vanguard, which would speed history along to fulfillment. Thus, while Communists everywhere believe that Communism is the next inevitable stage in history, they are not above precipitating the event.

It is in this area that the Communists pose a challenge to the West. The rise of nationalism in the dependencies of the Western European states has forced a liquidation of traditional empires. Undoubtedly, the empires would have decayed in time, but the rise of anti-colonial movements has speeded the transition to independence, and in many cases long before the colonial territory was prepared for full self-government.

Along with the nationalist movement, there have been demands of a sweeping nature for social change within the former dependencies. In many cases, the demand for independence and the demand for social change have gone hand in hand. Revolutionaries, trained in Moscow, have attempted to take over the direction of these revolutionary forces—and they promise the overthrow of imperial control, as well as the liquidation of the local ruling-landlord class.

It is said that such situations are ripe for Communism—but this depends to a considerable degree on what the West, and specifically the United States, is able to contribute. If the Communists have enjoyed a considerable degree of success in the lesser-developed areas of the world, it has been due in part to the failure of the West to understand and identify itself with the forces making for change. The path of economic development—even in the 20th century—need not be that which Soviet Russia has followed, nor need it necessarily be the 19th century way of the industrialized Western countries. The newly-emerging states should be encouraged to identify and pursue that type of development which best suits their own interests—and, with the support of the West, build toward a society whose long-range goals are predominantly harmonious with those of the West. There is no better way to forestall the efforts of the Communists.

On the other hand, within the Communist bloc itself, the West might attempt to create those conditions which stimulate further growth of diversity of interest. Above all, the West might exploit the nationalist tendencies within the countries of the bloc, as the Communists seek to exploit them elsewhere in the world. A step in this direction might be Western recognition of the Mongolian People's Republic.

Finally, whether or not the Heartland powers achieve their goal of world domination will depend to a very considerable extent on the strength of the Western powers, on the cohesion and unity of Western Europe, on the continuing growth of the United States, and on the development of the non-Western countries allied with the West. For surely their combined strength, both economic and military, continuing to surpass that of the Communist bloc, will do much to ensure the survival of the West, outweighing the advantages which possession of the Heartland and its resources gives to any hostile force.

CONCLUSION

Our narrative has dealt primarily with the borderlands between Russia and China. And, as events have unfolded, their role has changed with the circumstances. From zones of tension between Imperial Russia, Imperial China, Soviet Russia and Nationalist China, the borderlands have become, since the Communist revolution in China, zones of cooperation and stabilization. Their further economic development will undoubtedly strengthen the hold that the Communists have over them—and, in turn, they will contribute much to the overall Communist strength. Indeed, the role of the borderlands in the future Sino-Soviet relations may in some ways be as dramatic as that played in preceding centuries of Russo-Chinese competition and distrust. Whatever the future may bring, the lands of Asia, where Russia and China meet, will continue to fascinate us, and what is more, demand our awareness and understanding.

Appendix

Russo-Chinese International Boundary Treaties and Agreements

TREATIES instrumental in determining the present boundaries between the USSR, the CPR, and the MPR go back to the Treaty of Nerchinsk in 1689, which was the first treaty ever signed between China and a European country. The most recent alteration in the boundary occurred during World War II, when the Soviet government annexed the Tannu-Tuva People's Republic in 1944, a former province of Outer Mongolia (and thus of China), which had been theoretically independent since the latter part of the 1920's, but in a practical sense was no more than a Soviet satellite. There is a possibility of other adjustments in the future, particularly since Soviet maps differ from those of the Chinese Communists at a number of places along the Sino-Soviet-Mongolian border.

Treaties and agreements since 1689, which pertain to the boundary, are listed chronologically, by zones:

FAR EAST AND MONGOLIA

AUGUST, 1689. TREATY OF NERCHINSK.

Under the terms of the treaty, it was agreed that the boundary between the Russian and Chinese Empires would extend from the Argun River, continuing along the Amur to the mouth of one of its tributaries, the Kerbechi, thence along the Kerbechi to the outer

Khingan Mountains, i.e., along the Yablonovoi and Stanovoi Mountains, to the source of the Ud River, which flows into the Sea of Okhotsk. All of the southern slopes of the Stanovoi Mountains with rivers flowing into the Amur were to belong to China, while all northern slopes with rivers flowing to the north were ceded to Russia. The boundary through the Ud Valley was not decided, and it remained neutral territory. All Russian ostrogs (posts) on the Amur, including the Russian post at Albazin, were to be destroyed, and no Russian colonists were permitted to settle on Manchurian territory beyond the river. Those already established there had to leave or become Chinese citizens. In all, the Chinese ceded about 93,000 square miles to the Russians.

APRIL, 1727. RUSSO-CHINESE AGREEMENT IN PEKING.

The agreement specified that the frontier from the Bay of Ud to the Stanovoi Mountains would remain undecided as in the Treaty of Nerchinsk, owing to the lack of definite topographical information concerning the region; but elsewhere the boundary would be determined by a joint Russo-Chinese border commission.

OCTOBER, 1727. TREATY OF KIAKHTA.

Under the terms of the treaty, the boundary was fixed between Mongolia and Siberia, from the Sayan Mountains and Sapintabakha (Shaban-Dabeg), a pass through the Sayan in the west to the Argun River in the east (Article 3). The commission, however, was unclear in defining the border in the vicinity of Urianghai or Tuva. As far as the Russians were concerned, as they later were to claim, the allegiance of Tuva remained undetermined. Nevertheless, according to Count Sava Vladislavich Roguzinskii, the Russian envoy at Kiakhta, ". . . the newly established frontier is highly advantageous to Russia and . . . actually the Russian possessions have been extended into Mongolia a distance of several days' march, and, in certain sections, of even several weeks." For their part, the Chinese lost nearly 40,000 square miles, between the Upper Irtysh and the Sayan Mountains, as well as south and southwest of Lake Baikal. The boundary west of the Bay of Ud remained undefined (Article 7).

OCTOBER, 1768. KIAKHTA SUPPLEMENTARY TREATY.

Article 10 of the Treaty of Kiakhta was amended to regulate frontier traffic. Minor changes were also made in the vicinity of boundary posts.

MAY, 1858. TREATY OF AIGUN.

Under the terms of the treaty, Russia was ceded by China the left bank of the Amur down to the Ussuri, while the territory on the right bank as far as the Ussuri remained Chinese. The territory between the Ussuri and the Pacific Ocean was to belong in common to Russia and China until decided at a future date. In all, the Chinese surrendered to the Russians about 185,000 square miles of territory.

China was allowed to retain jurisdiction over the Manchu inhabitants on the left bank of the Amur from the Zeya River to the village of Khormoldsin, living in the "Sixty-Four Settlements to the East of the Amur," known as Chiang-Tung-Lu-Shih-Szu-T'un.

JUNE, 1858. TREATY OF TIENTSIN.

While the treaty was mainly commercial, it did include an article pertaining to the frontier. It stipulated that frontiers between the two powers not yet decided were to be surveyed. Actually, there was no need for this clause since the Treaty of Aigun embraced this point. However, it was included by the Russian negotiator because he was unaware at the time that the Aigun Treaty had been approved.

NOVEMBER, 1860. TREATY OF PEKING.

According to the treaty, the territory east of the Ussuri to the Pacific (133,000 square miles) was ceded to Russia (Article 1). The boundary between Russia and China was to follow the Ussuri south to and along its tributary, the Songatcha, thence across Lake Khanka to the Korean frontier. Delegates were to be appointed by the Chinese and Russian governments to survey and map the frontier from Lake Khanka to the Tumien River.

OCTOBER, 1864. BOUNDARY TREATY OF TARBAGATAI.

The treaty was concerned with the boundary between Sinkiang and Russian Turkestan, but it also referred to the Russian-Outer Mongolian boundary through the Sayan Mountains. This document was followed by an additional treaty in 1870, the Treaty of Uliassutai, which similarly referred to the demarcation of the Russian-Outer Mongolian boundary. Later, in 1911, when the question of Mongolia and Urianghai came up in cabinet discussions in St. Petersburg, Sazonov, the tsarist foreign minister reported that the Treaty of Tarbagatai (or Chuguchak) had clearly defined Urianghai as a part of Chinese territory.

DECEMBER, 1911. BOUNDARY TREATY BETWEEN RUSSIA AND CHINA, CON-CERNING THE BOUNDARY FROM TARBAGA DAGH TO ABAHAITU, AND ALONG THE ARGUN RIVER TO ITS CONFLUENCE WITH THE AMUR RIVER.

Under the terms of the treaty, commissions were appointed to fix precisely the international boundary.

NOVEMBER, 1913. NOTE TO THE CHINESE MINISTER FOR FOREIGN AFFAIRS, ON THE QUESTION OF OUTER MONGOLIAN AUTONOMY.

The Russian minister at Peking argued that Autonomous Outer Mongolia should comprise the regions which have been under the jurisdiction of the Chinese Amban of Urga; of the Tartar General of Uliassutai; and of the Chinese Amban of Kobdo. Inasmuch as there were no detailed maps of Mongolia, and as the boundaries of the administrative divisions of the country were uncertain, he agreed that the exact boundaries of Outer Mongolia, as well as the boundary between the district of Altai, should be the subject of the subsequent conferences provided for, in Article 5 of the Russo-Chinese Declaration of November 5, 1913.

JUNE, 1915. RUSSO-CHINESE-MONGOLIAN TRIPARTITE AGREEMENT.

Under Article 10 of the Agreement, the territory of Autonomous Outer Mongolia was said to comprise the regions which were under the jurisdiction of the Chinese Amban at Urga, of the Tartar-General at Uliassutai, and of the Chinese Amban at Kobdo. It connected with the boundary of China by the limits of the banners of the four aimaks of Khalka and of the district of Kobdo, bounded by the district of Houlunbouir (i.e., Hailar) on the east, by Inner Mongolia on the south, by the Province of Sinkiang on the southwest, and by the district of Altai on the west.

The formal delimitation between China and Autonomous Outer Mongolia was to be carried out by a special commission of delegates of China, Russia, and Autonomous Outer Mongolia, which would commence its work within a period of two years.

(In the struggle over Outer Mongolian "independence" in 1911, the westernmost Altai district had not been involved. Because of the loyalty to China of the Chinese governor there—and possibly because Russia preferred the Mongolian Altai Mountains as the western boundary of the autonomous state—Altai district was incorporated into Sinkiang in 1919.)

NOVEMBER, 1921. AGREEMENT FOR ESTABLISHING FRIENDLY RELATIONS BETWEEN SOVIET RUSSIA AND MONGOLIA.

Under the terms of the agreement, the frontier between Russia and Mongolia was to be established by a special commission, agreed to by the Russian Republic and Mongolia. However, Urianghai, the northwestern province of Mongolia, although claimed as part of its territory by Mongolia, was not acknowledged as such by the Russians.

MAY, 1924. AGREEMENT ON GENERAL PRINCIPLES FOR THE SETTLEMENT OF THE QUESTIONS BETWEEN THE REPUBLIC OF CHINA AND THE USSR.

Article 7 of the agreement pledged the two countries to redemarcate their national boundaries at a conference to be held within one month after the signing of the agreement; and, pending such redemarcation, to maintain their common boundary.

AUGUST, 1926. TREATY OF FRIENDSHIP BETWEEN THE PEOPLE'S REPUBLIC OF TANNU-TUVA AND THE MONGOLIAN PEOPLE'S REPUBLIC.

In the agreement, the governments, under Soviet pressure, recognized their separation and each other's independence. Because of

Outer Mongolia's opposition to the loss of Urianghai, the Soviets arranged to have Darkhat, a small, sparsely inhabited strip of territory west of Lake Khobso Gol, transferred, from Urianghai to Mongolia.

CENTRAL ASIA

NOVEMBER, 1860. TREATY OF PEKING.

The treaty, in those sections pertaining to Turkestan, specified that the boundary between Russia and China should be based upon the then-existing line of permanent pasture pickets, which the Chinese had established to limit the use of pastures by the nomadic Kazakhs. Commissioners were to be appointed by the Chinese and Russian governments to survey and map the frontier from Shaban-Dabeg to the Kokan's possessions (Kokand). In effect, China surrendered her claim to nearly 350,000 square miles.

OCTOBER, 1864. TREATY OF TARBAGATAI.

Under the terms of the treaty, which was hastily concluded because of an Islamic revolt in Sinkiang, the boundary was drawn along the line of permanent pickets, as agreed on at Peking in 1860.

(In attempting to regulate the use of pastures, China had established two types of pickets—permanent and movable. The Chinese commissioners contended that the boundary line should be drawn along the outermost, movable pickets, whereas the Russians insisted that it should follow the line of permanent pickets as provided in the Treaty of Peking. Thus, at Tarbagatai, the Chinese ceded extensive tracts of land, over which, however, they had held little more than a regulatory control.)

The boundary was, therefore, fixed as following the mountains, great rivers, and the existing line of Chinese permanent pickets. It ran from the light-house at Shaban-Dabeg southwestward to Lake Zaisan, thence to the mountains situated to the south of Lake Issyk-Kul and "along these mountains as far as the Kokan's possessions" (Article 2).

(Later, between 1869 and 1870, the boundary lines in the Kobdo,

Uliassutai, and Tarbagatai regions of Mongolia and Sinkiang, as noted above, were defined and boundary stakes set up. When, in 1870, the boundary was staked at Tarbagatai, the Russians planted some stakes in Chinese territory, intruding for another score of miles and cutting the main thoroughfare between Tarbagatai and Altai.)

FEBRUARY, 1881. TREATY OF ST. PETERSBURG.

(In July, 1870, the Russians occupied the upper Ili River Valley on the pretext of maintaining law and order during the local Islamic revolt against Chinese administration. The Chinese were unable to put down the revolt, or to compel the Russians to leave the Ili.

In July, 1879, in the Treaty of Livadia, signed by the Chinese delegate in St. Petersburg but never ratified by the Chinese government, the Chinese agreed under the terms of the treaty to cede the Tekes Valley and the strategic passes through the Tien-Shan, including the route to Kashgar. In return, Russia promised to withdraw from the rest of the Ili region.)

Under the terms of the Treaty of St. Petersburg, which was ratified by Peking, China retained the Tekes Valley and the passes through the Tien-Shan. However, a small area west of the Holkuts River was ceded to Russia (Article 7), for the purpose of settling the emigrants from Chinese Turkestan, that is, those inhabitants of the Chinese territory who preferred to live under Russian rule.

According to Article 8, the boundary lines east of Lake Zaisan and west of Kashgar, as determined by the Treaty of Tarbagatai, were to be redemarcated. (In the boundary agreements that followed: in August, 1862, concerning the southern boundary of the Ili; in November, 1882, concerning Kashgar; in July, 1883, concerning Kobdo and Tarbagatai; and in May, 1885, concerning Kashgar, China lost more than 15,000 square miles of territory to Russia.)

MARCH, 1895. AGREEMENT BETWEEN GREAT BRITAIN AND RUSSIA, WITH REGARD TO THE SPHERES OF INFLUENCE OF THE TWO COUNTRIES IN THE REGION OF THE PAMIRS.

(The Russian advance into Central Asia alarmed the British, who were concerned for the security of India. In 1873, however, the

Russians agreed to accept the course of the Amu-Darya [Oxus] between its source in Lake Zar-Kul in the Pamirs to a point where the river turns northward [near long. 66°E] as the northern boundary of Afghanistan. When the British withdrew from Afghanistan after the Second Afghan War, for all practical purposes Afghanistan became a buffer state between the two major powers.

In the meantime, after the Chinese had recovered control of Sinkiang, they established in 1878 their frontier posts in the Pamirs. But the rugged nature of the terrain prevented any precise demarcation.

In 1891, the tsar dispatched troops to the eastern Pamirs to protect Russian scientific expeditions. Alarmed by this new advance, Britain then invaded Hunza, a mountainous state southeast of Wakhan, owing allegiance to China. The Chinese government protested to no avail. In order to secure the northwest frontier of India against Russia, Britain made an effort to secure Chinese participation in a boundary agreement. Since no agreement was forthcoming, Britain and Russia came to terms on a Pamir boundary. Afghanistan, under British pressure, agreed to accept the narrow Wakhan Valley, which would thus prevent contiguity between Russia and British India.)

In the summer of 1895, according to the terms of the Anglo-Russian agreement of the preceding March, demarcation of the Russian-Afghanistan boundary took place. The line was drawn eastward from Lake Zar-Kul along the crest of mountains to the valley of the Ak-Su, thence eastward through the valley for two miles. From that point, it turned southeast for six miles, where it reached a rugged and inaccessible spur of the Sarikol Range.

Bibliography

A Regional Handbook on Northwest China, New Haven, HRAF Press, 1956, 2 vols.

Max Beloff, *Soviet Policy in the Far East,* 1944-51, London, Oxford University Press, 1953.

Howard L. Boorman and others, *Moscow-Peking Axis: Strengths and Strains,* New York, Harper & Bros., 1957.

Olaf Caroe, *Soviet Empire: The Turks of Central Asia and Stalinism,* London, Macmillan & Co., 1953.

Edward Hallett Carr, *The Bolshevik Revolution,* 1917-1923, Vol. 1, New York, Macmillan & Co., 1951.

Cheng Tien-fong, *A History of Sino-Soviet Relations,* Washington, Public Affairs Press, 1957.

George B. Cressey, *Land of the 500 Million: A Geography of China,* New York, McGraw-Hill Book Co., Ltd., 1955.

David J. Dallin, *Soviet Russia and the Far East,* New Haven, Yale University Press, 1948.

David J. Dallin, *The Rise of Russia in Asia,* New Haven, Yale University Press, 1949.

W. Gordon East and A. E. Moodie (eds.), *The Changing World: Studies in Political Geography,* London, George G. Harrap & Co., Ltd., 1956.

Louis Fischer, *The Soviets in World Affairs,* Princeton, Princeton University Press, 1951, 2 vols.

Gerard M. Friters, *Outer Mongolia and Its International Position,* Baltimore, Johns Hopkins University Press, 1949.

Elliot R. Goodman, *The Soviet Design for a World State,* New York, Columbia University Press, 1960.

Ho Ping-ti, *Studies on the Population of China, 1368-1953,* Cambridge, Mass., Harvard University Press, 1959.

Charles W. Hostler, *Turkism and the Soviets, New York,* Frederick A. Praeger, 1957.

Hsiao Hsia (ed.), *China: Its People, Its Society, Its Culture,* New Haven, HRAF Press, 1960.

G. F. Hudson and Marthe Rajchman, *An Atlas of Far Eastern Politics,* London, Faber and Faber Ltd., 1938.

George F. Kennan, *Russia and the West under Lenin and Stalin,* Boston, Little, Brown & Co., 1961.

Walter Kolarz, *Russia and Her Colonies,* London, George Phillips & Son Ltd., 1952.

Walter Kolarz, *The Peoples of the Soviet Far East,* New York, Frederick A. Praeger, 1954.

Owen Lattimore, *The Mongols of Manchuria,* New York, The John Day Co., 1934.

Owen Lattimore, *Manchuria: Cradle of Conflict,* 2nd ed., New York, Macmillan & Co., 1935.

Owen Lattimore, *Inner Asian Frontiers of China,* New York, American Geographical Society, 1940, 1951.

Owen Lattimore, *Nationalism and Revolution in Mongolia,* New York, Oxford University Press, 1955.

Prince A. Lobanov-Rostovsky, *Russia and Asia,* Ann Arbor, G. Wahr Publ. Co., 1951. (Originally published by Macmillan, N.Y., 1933.)

Lionel W. Lyde, *The Continent of Asia,* London, Macmillan & Co., 1933.

Sir Halford J. Mackinder, *Democratic Ideals and Reality. A Study in the Politics of Reconstruction,* New York, Henry Holt & Co., 1919, 1942.

Manchuria. Treaties and Agreements, Washington, Carnegie Endowment for International Peace, 1921.

William M. McGovern, *The Early Empires of Central Asia,* Chapel Hill, University of North Carolina Press, 1939.

Alexandre Metaxas, *Pekin Contre Moscou,* Lausanne, Editions Scriptar, 1959.

Franz H. Michael and George E. Taylor, *The Far East in the Modern World,* New York, Henry Holt & Co., 1956.

Mongolian People's Republic, New Haven, HRAF Press, 1956, 3 vols.

Outer Mongolia. Treaties and Agreements, Washington, Carnegie Endowment for International Peace, 1921.

Alexander G. Park, *Bolshevism in Turkestan, 1917-1927,* New York, Columbia University Press, 1957.

Richard A. Pierce, *Russian Central Asia, 1867-1917,* Berkeley and Los Angeles, University of California Press, 1960.

Richard Pipes, *The Formation of the Soviet Union: Communism and*

Nationalism, 1917-1923 Cambridge, Mass., Harvard University Press, 1954.

Harrison E. Salisbury, *To Moscow—and Beyond,* New York, Harper & Bros., 1959.

Theodore Shabad, *Geography of the USSR, A Regional Survey,* New York, Columbia University Press, 1951.

Theodore Shabad, *China's Changing Map,* New York, Frederick A. Praeger, 1956.

Peter S. H. Tang, *Communist China Today,* New York, Frederick A. Praeger, 1957, 1958, 2 vols.

Peter S. H. Tang, *Russian and Soviet Policy in Manchuria and Outer Mongolia, 1911-1931,* Durham, Duke University Press, 1959.

John E. Tashjean, *Where China Meets Russia: An Analysis of Dr. Starlinger's Theory,* Central Asian Collectanea, No. 2, Washington, 1959.

The Travels of Marco Polo, New York, Boni and Liveright, 1926.

Erich Thiel, *The Soviet Far East, A Survey of Its Physical and Economic Geography,* New York, Frederick A. Praeger, 1957.

Treaties and Agreements with and Concerning China, 1894-1919, Washington, Carnegie Endowment for International Peace, 1921, 2 vols.

Treaties and Agreements with and Concerning China, 1919-1929, Washington, Carnegie Endowment for International Peace, 1929.

Hans W. Weigert and others, *Principles of Political Geography,* New York, Appleton-Century-Crofts, 1957.

Allen S. Whiting, *Soviet Policies in China, 1917-1924,* New York, Columbia University Press, 1954.

Allen S. Whiting and General Sheng Shih-ts'ai, *Sinkiang: Pawn or Pivot?* East Lansing, Michigan State University Press, 1958.

Aitchen K. Wu, *China and the Soviet Union. A Study of Sino-Soviet Relations,* New York, The John Day Co., 1950.

Victor A. Yakhontoff, *Russia and the Soviet Union in the Far East,* London, Allen & Unwin, 1932.

C. Walter Young, *The International Relations of Manchuria,* Chicago, University of Chicago Press, 1929.

Index

123

79

DATE DUE

APR 10 '78			
MAY 2 1984			
		.	